A Handbook of
Children's Grief

A HANDBOOK OF CHILDREN'S GRIEF

For Adults Supporting Children

Atle Dyregrov
and Martin Lytje

Jessica Kingsley Publishers
London and Philadelphia

First edition published in Norway in 2021 by Vigmostad & Bjørke
First published in the English language in Great Britain
in 2024 by Jessica Kingsley Publishers
An imprint of John Murray Press

1

Front cover image source: iStockphoto®.

A CIP catalogue record for this title is available from the
British Library and the Library of Congress

ISBN 978 1 80501 169 9
eISBN 978 1 80501 170 5

Printed and bound in Great Britain by CPI Group

Jessica Kingsley Publishers' policy is to use papers that are natural,
renewable and recyclable products and made from wood grown in
sustainable forests. The logging and manufacturing processes are expected
to conform to the environmental regulations of the country of origin.

Jessica Kingsley Publishers
Carmelite House
50 Victoria Embankment
London EC4Y 0DZ

www.jkp.com

John Murray Press
Part of Hodder & Stoughton Ltd
An Hachette Company

Contents

Introduction: A Journey from Grief in Adults to Grief in Children

In 1981, Philippe Ariès, a renowned French historian, penned *The Hour of Our Death*, a significant work that explores humanity's relationship with death throughout history. It is widely considered one of the greatest books on the topic, and Ariès highlights the pervasive and enduring influence of death in the rise and fall of civilizations. Ancient monuments like the Colosseum in Rome, the pyramids in Egypt, and Viking graves in Scandinavia provide evidence of how people in the past related to death. Having lasted until today, these monuments reveal how societies have always had a fundamental need to understand, categorize, and describe death. Additionally, works from the Greeks, Romans, and medieval theologians demonstrate past generations' efforts to interpret the phenomenon of death, further emphasizing its importance throughout history.

In the 1800s and 1900s, the study of death as an academic field gained momentum with contributions from famous personalities such as philosophers Søren Kierkegaard and Friedrich Nietzsche, as well as psychiatrists Sigmund Freud, John Bowlby, and Elisabeth Kübler-Ross. This led to various philosophical works, psychological theories, and practical models aimed at characterizing and defining death and the accompanying dilemmas. Despite disagreements about the nature of death and grief, all of these figures agreed that death is one of the most profound, challenging, and life-changing experiences that people can undergo.

In this view, it is paradoxical that, with the exception of Bowlby, the same individuals who addressed adult grief seldom addressed the grief of children. While there have been philosophical inquiries into adult grief since the advent of written works, the grief of children has historically been neglected. Its study did not receive significant attention until the beginning of the 20th century. Even then, it was often approached as research done *to* children, not *with* children. The prevalent notion was that children could not experience grief as they lacked the understanding of death.

Research including children's perspectives first really gained prominence in the 1990s. Prior to this, the ethical concerns that arose in dealing with children's grief were often considered too overwhelming to tackle. Some saw it as inferior to adult grief and best dealt with within the privacy of the home. Fortunately, these attitudes no longer exist in the research community. Children's grief has become a small but distinct field of study. However, despite the advancements made in our understanding, there are still many questions that remain unanswered.

About this book

This book is intended as a qualifying work and a guide for anyone who encounters children's grief, whether you are a teacher, an educator, a psychologist, or a concerned family member. Although some sections are written more specifically for school support or therapy and are thus more relevant to some professionals, we believe that all the chapters in this book can help you gain a more comprehensive understanding of children's grief. Perhaps more importantly, this book highlights how you can support the child in all the areas where grief can affect them and their lives. As such, even if you are not a teacher, it is still relevant to understand where the challenges for bereaved children may arise in school, and what issues you can help teachers to focus on.

In recent years, many books have been published on the subject of children's grief. Some of these books examine the scientific advancements in our understanding of how children cope with loss, while others feature narratives from adults who lost loved ones during their childhood. A third category of these books provides guidance and support for professionals who work with grieving children. Despite the wealth of information contained in these publications, it is uncommon to find a book that brings together all of these perspectives. This handbook of children's grief aims to do just that, by encompassing a comprehensive and multifaceted approach to this complex experience. To do this, the book draws on scientific research, clinical experience, and stories and quotes from bereaved children, and offers practical and concrete advice for supporting their grief.

Both authors of this book work as researchers and psychologists specializing in this field. Although we are at different places in our respective careers, we have dedicated our lives to understanding children's grief and need for support. The aim of our book is to equip you with the necessary knowledge, courage, and insight to confidently support a child facing one of the most challenging times of their life. Research has shown that the involvement of a supportive adult at a time when a child faces a difficult life situation can make an important difference. By taking on this supportive task, you can help the child navigate their grief.

What is grief?

Ariès (1981) describes how loss is shaped by the times we live in and the relationship we have with the deceased – both as individuals and as a society. Grief and loss are thus not a static quality, but shaped by the type of loss, the survivor's social situation, and the society in which the bereaved lives.

Defining grief is a complex issue, and it has become even more demanding with the introduction by the World Health Organization and the American Psychiatric Association of a distinction between 'ordinary grief' and other forms of grief, through their classification of prolonged grief disorder. However, since these diagnoses have not been thoroughly tested on children, who are the focus of this book, we will not be discussing these specific diagnoses in depth. If you would like to learn more about our perspectives on complicated grief reactions in children and the support initiatives we recommend, please refer to Chapter 6.

The question remains: 'So how do we define grief in this book?' We see grief as the natural emotions and reactions a child experiences at the loss of a loved one. In the book, we define a loved one as an important person in the child's relational life, such as a mother, father, sibling, or friend. Although children naturally also grieve the loss of grandparents or pets, we see such losses as something that families in the vast majority of cases have the capacity to deal with themselves. However, it is important to say that the experience of loss is always individual, and in some cases the loss of a grandparent who had a central role in the child's life may be more difficult than the loss of a father or mother who was never there. Therefore, as a support person, you should always start from the individual loss and base your support on the needs you see in the child. Here you will often be able to apply our advice, even if the topic we are writing about is parents or siblings.

We hope that this book will contribute to increased knowledge and better help for children who have lost a loved one, although we admit that there still is much to learn about children's grief.

Chapter 1

Grief Reactions in Children

Introduction: Understanding the diversity of children's grief reactions

Through our years of experience, we've learned that there's no one 'right' way for children to react to death. Every child is unique, and their reactions are influenced by a range of factors, including their backgrounds, experiences, and home environments. Through illness, children may be exposed to parents who gradually disappear from their everyday lives, while sudden deaths – often dramatic with children as witnesses – can abruptly turn their everyday lives upside down. Experiences with the deceased can range from loving care to daily fear of abuse or mistreatment. Don't forget that children are met afterwards by adults – at home, at nursery, and at school – who react in many ways and treat them very differently. The same is true with friends and acquaintances, who also act in distinct ways in terms of understanding and ability to support. There are many circumstances that vary from child to child, and it is not unusual for children to react differently. Despite this, it is possible to highlight some responses that are more common than others – although it is difficult to say that any particular reaction shortly after the loss is unusual.

Some children may grieve intensely and immediately, while

others may take longer to process their emotions. Some may exhibit anger or other challenging behaviours, while others may withdraw and show no outward signs of sadness. As psychologists with years of experience working with children, young people, and adults in grief, we have encountered an astonishing range of reactions and coping mechanisms. It is important to recognize and validate each child's individual journey through grief, even if their response does not align with our own experiences or expectations.

In this chapter, we describe the most common reactions that many children experience, which can be expressed in different ways. Whatever the reactions, we must try to understand them, accept them, and affirm them, even though we may not have met that particular way of expressing grief in the past. It is thought-provoking for us that more than 50% of teenagers (according to a Swedish study) did not find a good way to grieve in the first six months after the loss of a parent (Bylund-Grenklo *et al.*, 2021).

Common grief reactions

It can be incredibly difficult for children to comprehend and make sense of their reactions to grief. They're entering new and unfamiliar terrain for which they have no map to navigate, leaving them feeling lost and unsure of how to proceed. As they continue to develop and grow, children may revisit their grief, reflect on it, and learn new things, or find themselves struggling with situations that others find easier to cope with. It takes patience and understanding to follow children through their grief journey, especially given the fact that some adults tend to overlook the long-term impact of grief on children.

It's not uncommon for adults to assume that children will eventually be fine as time passes and they grow older, but this perspective overlooks the fact that grief can take on new and unexpected forms as children mature and develop their own understanding of what happened and how it has affected them. In some cases, new knowledge or insights can be even more challenging for children to process, leading them to blame themselves for not doing more to prevent the loss, for example.

To help shed light on some of the normal grief reactions that are commonly observed in the aftermath of a parental loss, we will review some of these reactions in the following section. It's important to note, however, that these are not always seen, and that grief can manifest in many different ways for different children.

Unreality and shock

When serious illness strikes the family, children's reactions will usually reflect how they have been informed about the illness and its seriousness. If they understand that their mother or father may die from the disease, they may experience it as unreal, yet take this knowledge on board and become very frightened. Often they oscillate between unreality and responses such as sadness and anxiety about what might happen. If the child is not informed that a disease process could potentially lead to a death, there will be more anxiety but less strong reactions. If the child only gets limited information or disregards the information about the seriousness of the illness, the shock is often delayed and only hits when the child sees for themselves what the illness leads to.

In sudden deaths, the mind will often put the brakes on quite immediately, and many children, especially from school age upwards, will experience a sense of unreality. They may not believe it's true.

'I didn't understand it. Everything was a bit like a dream. I couldn't believe it was true, that it was about Mum. I didn't want to believe it either. So, I just pushed it away.' *Elise, aged 13, who lost her mother*

It's no wonder that the mind has a protective mechanism that lets people understand what's happened, little by little. This is especially necessary if there is no time for mental preparation for what is happening, for example in the case of death as a result of an accident, suicide, or acute illness. Some children protest loudly, while others react with apathy and paralysis. Adults may misinterpret children's lack of an immediate response as a failure to comprehend the reality of the situation, leading to confusion when a child asks to go and play after receiving news of a death. Some children may even try to comfort others, despite needing comfort themselves, and blame themselves for not responding 'enough'. Understanding the variety of reactions that children may exhibit and their underlying causes is important in supporting them during times of crisis.

In Chapter 8 (Grief in the Family), we write about a teenager who suddenly loses her mother and becomes very angry with her cousin, who responds more visibly than she does during the funeral. She does not understand how feelings of unreality have temporarily dampened her reactions. Adults who explain to children early on why they are responding in a certain way can prevent unnecessary self-recrimination about under-reacting. It is fortunate that we humans have a 'shock response' that allows us to gradually come to terms with traumatic events, so that the reality of the situation does not become too overwhelming all at once.

Yearning and longing

Many people experience strong emotions when they realize what has happened, while others continue to keep their reactions at bay because the 'anaesthetic' of the shock keeps the longing away. Younger children in particular are not good at emotion regulation and are rarely sad about it for long periods. They go in and out of grief and use activities to break difficult emotions. When strong feelings of missing and longing for the deceased arise, it can activate the 'braking mechanisms' that dampen the pain, and they can alternate between strong feelings and an experience of unreality. Longing means a strong desire for the unattainable lost person.

Children may attempt to conceal their sadness so as not to upset their parents, and when they do cry, they may claim that it's because of something unrelated to the death, such as a headache. Grief reminders are situations that trigger the child's grief, such as seeing an empty chair where the deceased used to sit, hearing a song that the deceased enjoyed on the radio, or visiting the grave site. The happiness of others can also trigger feelings of loss and longing, especially if they observe other children doing things with a parent or sibling that they wish they could do themselves. Some children may actively seek out places and situations that they used to frequent with the deceased because it makes them feel closer to them, while others may spend a lot of time reminiscing.

> A mother of a nursery-age child noticed that her son watched videos of his late father repeatedly for several hours each day. She asked a psychologist if this behaviour was normal. The psychologist advised the mother that this behaviour was a way for the child to create an inner image of his father, who used to be present in his environment every day but was now suddenly gone. By watching the videos, the child was able to keep him close to his heart, even though he was no longer physically present in everyday life. The mother was advised to allow her son time to engage in this activity, as it was a healthy coping mechanism for the child's grief.

Young children often try to fill the void left by their deceased loved one by seeking out their presence in various ways. For instance, a two-and-a-half-year-old boy who had lost his baby sister frequently visited her empty bed and called her name. Children use different methods such as looking at pictures and watching videos searching for familiar places, or keeping something that belonged to the deceased close to them, to create a sense of connection with the person who has died. These behaviours are usually most prominent in the immediate aftermath of the death. On the other hand, some children may find it too painful to engage in such activities and choose to avoid them altogether. However, as we discuss in Chapter 7 (Coping with Loss), an avoidant coping style can often lead to more difficulties in dealing with grief. Children and adolescents commonly experience a sense of having a continued relationship or a continuing bond and may feel the presence of the lost parent, which can help their transition from having the parent's physical presence to only having memories. However, excessive preoccupation with the deceased may disrupt current relationships and functioning (Clabburn *et al.*, 2021; Sirrine *et al.*, 2018).

During the course of grief, usually the pain diminishes over time, the outbursts subside, and everyday life becomes more normal; but reminders of both grief and trauma can quickly produce intense longing. Reminders of trauma are understood here as a re-experiencing of parts or all of the event, triggered by sensations that remind the affected child of the trauma event. It may be sounds, smells, and other impressions, such as a sound reminiscent of a ventilator, ambulance sirens, or the sight of blood. This is a natural part of a child's grieving process and can be a way for the child to process their own grief and then turn to other activities. Here, actions such as a grief box with objects, pictures, and the perfume of the deceased can help create a space where the child can remember and grieve.

Post-traumatic reactions

Reminders of trauma often trigger post-traumatic reactions, where uninvited memories resurface and the situation is re-lived. When such reactions occur after the death of a parent, they often reflect episodes that were highly stressful during the course of the illness or at the time of death. These may include memories of a relapse in the disease, episodes in hospital, or other circumstances associated with particular moments during the course of the illness. Re-experiences and intrusive memories are most common after sudden deaths and are triggered by memories of the death itself – e.g., the ambulance, the ambulance helicopter, the health staff – or images and text from media reports of similar incidents. Memories can be linked to specific sensory experiences in different sensory channels, which come uninvited into thoughts.

> In one instance of sudden death at home, a mother let out uncontrollable screams on finding the deceased. Her daughter, who was barely ten years old at the time, was present and the screams became firmly fixed in her memory. For a period following the loss, loud screams and anything resembling them immediately triggered the memory of what had happened, which was a heavy burden for her. However, through gradual exposure therapy where she listened to shouts and screams with increasing volume and intensity from a computer, her reactions gradually subsided.
>
> Another girl had a brother who hanged himself in their house. She was present when they found him, and in the time afterwards the sight of ropes triggered haunting memories. She reacted when her peers used jumping ropes, and unfortunately someone discovered that they could make her react by showing her a rope, and teased her with it. Children can be mean to each other at times. Advice on gradual exposure, and a mother who took action, improved the situation.

For the majority of children, initial post-traumatic reactions tend to subside within the first few days and weeks following the traumatic event. However, if this is not the case, it is important that the child receives prompt intervention to manage and gain control over their memories. The post-traumatic responses can impede the grieving process as they may trigger traumatic memories whenever the child's thoughts turn towards the deceased.

Another post-traumatic reaction that children may experience is losing faith in their future. They may harbour thoughts such as not living to adulthood, dying early, or facing other adversities. These thoughts can cause anxiety for those close to the child. In such cases, psychological support may be necessary to ease and process these distressing thoughts.

Guilt and self-blame

It is easy for children to blame themselves. Especially among younger children aged four to ten, the understanding of the cause is less nuanced. They may think that things happen because they wanted or desired them to (e.g., if in anger they wanted a sibling or parent to go away), or they may have an incorrect perception of what led to what.

> One young girl, whose mother had taken her own life, believed it was her fault because she was always angry and grumpy. Children who are grieving may feel guilty for various reasons, such as not grieving enough, not doing something they think they should have, or not thinking about the deceased enough. They may judge their own reactions harshly because they have little experience with grief. Children may also oscillate between mourning and taking breaks away from their grief, smiling and laughing shortly after the death and not constantly having the deceased in mind, which can lead to feelings of guilt. Additionally, thoughtless remarks from others can intensify their reaction, and even well-meaning comments, such as 'I think you're so great and taking it so well,' may be interpreted by the child as [their] not grieving enough or not thinking enough about the deceased.

Here is a list of examples of what children can feel guilt about in the context of death:

- Not grieving enough or being too quickly 'over' their grief.

- Not visiting the grave often enough or thinking enough about the deceased.

- Saying or doing things to the deceased while they were alive – or failing to say or do things.

- Not understanding how the deceased felt before their death (especially in the case of suicide).

- Feeling fine themselves while the deceased cannot experience the same.

- Failing to act, or knowing things and not speaking out – things they think could have prevented what happened.

- Not being able to remember details about the deceased, such as their eye colour or how they smelled.

Most often, children feel guilty when they have done nothing wrong, and their guilt is based on misunderstandings or lack of knowledge. However, there are situations where they may genuinely be responsible for a negative outcome, such as luring a younger sibling onto thin ice, resulting in drowning, or distracting a parent while driving, which lead to an accident.

> A teenage boy felt guilty for being rude to his mother, who passed away due to cancer. He had sworn at her a few times, and he was plagued with thoughts of whether she was very upset and believed that he did not love her. It was necessary to explain to him how common it is for emotions to become inflamed during adolescence and that strong words can often be used against those one is fond of. He was advised to visit his mother's graveside, apologize, and talk to her. He was encouraged to express how much he loved and appreciated her, and that she would always be in his heart.

Self-reproach is a natural response following critical events because it allows us to reflect and learn from important situations. By considering alternative courses of action, we broaden our experience and may be better prepared for future challenges. However, if self-blame persists with great intensity beyond the first few weeks, it can interfere with children's daily functioning. Brooding or ruminating can be particularly detrimental. While it is important to reassure children that they are not at fault, simply telling them to stop thinking negatively may not be enough. It's important to understand how children think and to help them shift their thoughts in a positive direction. This may involve providing additional information, reassurance, and guidance.

Sometimes it is possible to calm such self-blaming feelings by asking challenging questions, but this requires the child to be old enough to be able to understand the following questions:

- 'Did you know enough to prevent the death before it happened, or are you criticizing yourself for something you were only told afterwards?'

- 'If a friend had said what you are saying now, what would you think?'

- 'Can you see into the future, since you are criticizing yourself for something you only found out afterwards?'

Up to the age of about six, children tend to view the world through an egocentric lens, often attributing events to their own actions. At these ages, their cognitive development is still such that they have difficulty distinguishing between reality and fantasy. This can cause young children to need assistance from adults to grasp the fact that some of their actions and thoughts are not capable of causing death or accidents.

School-age children may also be advised to set aside a fixed time each day to address such thoughts. This is a strategy that can be used for all kinds of thoughts that cause anxiety and worry. If thoughts come up outside the time allocated, children should tell themselves: 'I notice that I am starting to think about this now, but I will wait for my "thinking time".' This can allow the thoughts time to stop automatically, and the need for the thinking time will diminish. Children should be told that it is normal for these thoughts to occur and they should try not to get annoyed with themselves, but simply postpone the thoughts. Finally, children can be prompted to ask themselves what the deceased would have said to them if they heard them blame themselves. Very few will say that the deceased person would have wanted them to feel hurt in that way.

Anxiety and fear

One of the most common reactions seen after a death is anxiety and fear. Children experience that life changes from being safe to being a place where terrible things can happen. If children have lost a parent, their biggest fear is that something will happen to their remaining parent. Young children may cling to them and fear separation for a long time. If asked, a child will often admit to having 'silly thoughts' that something will happen to their surviving parent.

The circumstances of the death can also intensify fears related to activities that in some way parallel the death. For instance, if it occurred in a traffic accident, children may become wary when the surviving parent has to go out driving. If the death was related to a brain tumour that began as a headache, children can become very frightened if their remaining parent experiences a headache. The anxiety may also arise when they are at school and have little control over what happens at home, or when they have to sit still and do their homework.

Fear of death is a common and understandable reaction for children who have experienced the loss of a loved one. While this fear is often most intense in relation to the surviving parent, children may also become afraid of dying themselves, especially when going to sleep at night. This fear can be worsened by the association between death, darkness, and sleep, which can create a sense of vulnerability and helplessness.

In addition to fearing for their own life, children may also experience anxiety about the potential loss of other important people in their lives, such as siblings or grandparents. While the fear of disasters happening may gradually dissipate over time, some children continue to struggle with persistent and distressing anxiety, which can be challenging for them to manage without proper support and guidance.

Fear can also manifest in a different form, where the child becomes afraid of forgetting the deceased parent. They may worry about suddenly not remembering details such as how the parent looked, laughed, spoke, or smelled. In such cases, a bereavement box containing pictures and objects of the deceased, such as perfume, jewellery, or video footage, can be a beneficial way to ease their anxiety.

To help children cope with their fears, it is important to acknowledge that their feelings are normal and understandable. Talking to someone they trust, such as a familiar adult or a bereavement group, can help alleviate the intrusiveness of their fears. Parents or surviving parents can also reassure children by communicating their whereabouts and availability, and by emphasizing that one death does not increase the likelihood of another. While it is impossible to guarantee that nothing else will happen, children will gradually discover that such events are rare and they will learn to relax over time.

Young children may sometimes misinterpret situations and as a consequence react with fear. This is what happened in the following example.

> A three-year-old boy witnessed his younger sister's sudden death. The mother had taken the sister to the hospital where she died that same day. Following the loss of his sister, the boy's behaviour changed. He began to distance himself from his mother and preferred to interact only with his father. The boy believed that the mother was responsible for his sister's death and became afraid that he too would meet the same fate.

Although the heightened anxiety typically lessens with time, some children may continue to experience it into adulthood and may develop a persistent fear of loss. Additionally, research has indicated that individuals who have experienced a parent dying at an early age (i.e., before the age of 55) may not believe they will live as long as those who have not experienced such loss (Denes-Raj & Ehrlichman, 1991).

Anger

Anger can come as a reaction following any type of death and can manifest itself throughout childhood and adolescence as:

- blame and anger towards the person or people the child perceives as responsible for the death

- anger towards individuals whom the child believes could have prevented the death, such as healthcare professionals, police, or a parent

- anger and a feeling of exclusion at being left out of important information or rituals related to the loss

- anger at themselves for not acting or thinking differently, which could have potentially prevented the death or allowed more time with the deceased

- resentfulness and anger towards the deceased or 'the world' for leaving the child alone

- frustration or anger towards friends who may not fully comprehend or empathize with the child's experience of loss.

When children experience the loss of a loved one, they may struggle with feelings of anger and frustration towards their environment. This can manifest as increased irritability and unruly behaviour towards friends and schoolmates, which may be compounded by disruptions to sleep and energy levels. Additionally, anger may play a role in family dynamics following a loss. For instance, in the case of parents who have lost a child, the anger and acting out of surviving siblings can help keep parents from becoming too consumed by grief. In some cases, such behaviour may even be deliberate, as a child seeks to spur a grieving parent into action.

> A boy who lived on an island where most residents were fishermen found that his father was spending a lot of time on the couch following the death of the boy's younger sister. In an effort to activate his father, the boy cut the moorings of several fishing boats in the harbour, forcing his father to get up and participate in their salvage. As the boy put it, 'I had to save him from death.'

The anger experienced by a grieving child may stem from a sense of unfairness, such as the belief that the death should not have happened to their particular family, or simply from the fact that the death occurred at all. Whatever the reason, these reactions often have a profound effect on those closest to the child, including siblings and parents.

It's important to note that anger in children following a loss can be directed towards various individuals and groups. For instance, it may be directed at health or emergency services staff, whom the child holds responsible for the death. In some cases, children may be angry with friends whom they believe should have foreseen and prevented the death, or who simply do not understand how they feel. Furthermore, anger can also be directed at teachers, particularly if they fail to acknowledge the child's grief or provide adequate support.

> Charlie, an 11-year-old boy, struggled with intense anger towards his teacher after his father's death, feeling that she didn't understand how much he was hurting. Despite a conversation with the teacher about his feelings, Charlie continued to feel overlooked

and neglected. He even had violent fantasies of blowing up the school and killing the teacher. It was important for Charlie to receive help in regulating these intense feelings. One way he learned to cope was by imagining his father's voice reaching out to him and offering reassurance. He would use 'strong thoughts' where his father would say things like, 'You can get through this,' 'Take it easy,' or, 'Teachers have short memories, but I will always be there for you to help you.'

When children experience the loss of a loved one, they may direct their anger towards insensitive teachers, parents, or other individuals they come into contact with. In the case of a killing, anger towards the perpetrator can be particularly strong. Boys, in particular, may express their sadness through anger – and sometimes can only let the tears flow when they are really angry. In such cases, calm adults are needed who can meet their reaction with patience and understanding. Excessive and uncontrollable anger such as hitting or kicking needs to be stopped, but here too a calm adult can act as a brake on the situation.

After suicide, mixed emotions can arise, with children at first just feeling sadness about the person who died, but later expressing anger at the person for what he or she did. They may thus express both despair and anger: 'Wasn't I worth living for?' It is important to stress that it is not the case that everyone will feel anger towards someone who takes their own life at some point, but many may experience anger that only surfaces much later.

Although anger is a common reaction, it is an emotion that creates discomfort for both the environment and the child themselves. And while adults should set limits on anger if it is directed at others, it is important to find ways for a child to express frustration and anger that are adapted to their age and maturity. Here is some advice:

- Notice when the anger comes and what it is related to. Help the child recognize the feeling in order to change it.

- Try to reduce the anger by enabling the child to express it by drawing or writing about it and what provokes it. In this way, the child can better control their feelings and thoughts.

- Talking to an adult is often the first step towards better control. If this does not work, professional help from a nurse or psychologist may be considered.

- Simple advice can be given: take a break, count to ten, walk away from the situation, breathe deeply in through the nose and out slowly through the mouth (or similar exercises).

- In addition, as in the example of Charlie, if the child can practise repeating strong thoughts that calm them down, such as 'I'm going to wait a bit, sit down, and talk calmly', they can gradually gain more control.

- Engage the child in physical activity, such as going for a walk, or playing football, netball, basketball, or similar.

- Help the child to learn the importance of taking responsibility for their actions and apologizing when they have hurt someone, as this can repair and maintain relationships.

When children behave unacceptably, it's important to establish boundaries. It's best to wait until the child has calmed down before initiating a conversation. Encourage them to share what happened or what they're finding difficult, or to express their thoughts and feelings in writing.

Sleep disorders

Sleep patterns can provide a useful indication of how children are coping with the loss of a loved one. Restless sleep, frequent waking, and unsettling dreams and nightmares are common after a death. While nightmares may sometimes re-enact the events, they often involve unrelated, frightening scenarios. Many children seek additional comfort by sharing a bed with a surviving parent or guardian, creating a sense of mutual support and security. However, it is important for adults to recognize this and gently encourage children to resume their own sleeping arrangements. Delaying bedtime or staying up too late can exacerbate sleep issues, which can affect school performance and daily life.

Children often struggle to fall asleep as thoughts and emotions surface more frequently in the quiet, dark environment when lying down. Worry and longing take over, causing restlessness and disrupting sleep. Simple distraction techniques, such as counting down from 100 or 1000 in fives or sevens (adapted to age and cognitive capacity), talking to parents, listening to quiet music, and venting worries earlier in the day may be helpful.

It's important to determine if sleep problems are related to trauma, which may require therapeutic treatment (as discussed in Chapter 6, Complicated Grief Processes). If intrusive memories or thoughts of the death are causing sleep problems, it's essential to address and reduce them early on.

Concentration and memory

Grief can impact a child's ability to concentrate and remember things. They may struggle to concentrate at school or at home, become pensive, and lose focus while attempting to remember, sometimes for an extended period. If the death has occurred after a long period of illness, they may have forgotten much of what happened during that period, or their memory may be poor for the period around the death and afterwards. The various reactions of grief and longing or guilt may, separately or together, intrude on thoughts, as may intrusive memories or thoughts.

As an adult supporting a grieving child, it's important to be patient with their decreased focus and forgetfulness. For older children, writing things down on paper or using a note-taking app on their phone can help with memory. It's also important to ask if the child is experiencing any troubling images or fantasies related to the loss. If these issues persist beyond the first three to five weeks, they are unlikely to resolve on their own and could interfere with the child's schooling. Early intervention is crucial in these cases.

Social interaction

Bereaved children may be marked by their loss, and this kind of thing is noticed by friends. Initially, friends can offer much warmth and care, and many also provide good support over time. However, as time goes on, peers may return to their normal lives and forget about their friend's loss. This can cause feelings of loneliness and being different, which may lead children to try to keep up appearances even though they feel a sense of loss and isolation. They may also withdraw from social situations because of the stark contrast between their lives and those of their peers. For example, it can be painful to hear someone talk about seeing their dad when you can no longer experience that yourself. It's important for adults to be aware of this and provide support to help grieving children feel included and supported in social contexts.

The new-life situation following a bereavement can sometimes result in the loss of closeness with friends, either due to relocation or the need to be more at home in order to support parents and younger siblings. In some cases, peers may say things that are not helpful or supportive, leading to feelings of being misunderstood or left out. Moreover, children who experience loss may mature faster than their peers, which can further increase feelings of loneliness and alienation. Research has shown that it can also be hard for friends to know how to navigate the child's grief and provide appropriate support. To address this, teachers or educators can gather the bereaved child's closest friends for a conversation on how to be a good friend and to establish a framework for how and when to talk about what has happened.

Participating in a grief group with other children who have

experienced loss can help alleviate the sense of being different and provide feelings of kinship. It can be beneficial for children to meet others in the same situation, learn that their reactions are normal, and receive advice on how to cope with difficult emotions and situations.

Other reactions

Physical complaints such as headaches, upset stomachs, and muscle aches are not uncommon reactions, and often these occur more frequently if the child responds less expressively or avoids dealing with their feelings. Either way, over time it is difficult to know whether the discomfort is the onset of illness or reflects an increased focus on physical reactions. If a parent or sibling dies of illness, symptoms similar to those experienced by the deceased may be particularly distressing for parent(s) and child.

The child may also experience regression in their development, which can be difficult to understand for the surviving parent. For example, a child who has stopped using a nappy may start wetting their pants again, or their language skills may temporarily deteriorate. In addition, they may behave more childishly than before the loss, which can be stressful for the parent who is grieving themselves. It's important for parents to approach these reactions with patience, even though it can be difficult when they also are dealing with their own grief.

Sometimes children may become preoccupied with thinking about what happened at the time of the death, and this can persist even as they mature and gain new perspectives on the situation. While children can learn techniques to manage these thoughts, if they continue to persist, it may be necessary to seek professional help. In addition to brooding, some children may develop a pessimistic outlook on the future and may even experience depression before reaching adolescence. While grief is focused on the loss of the deceased, depression is characterized by a more general feeling of hopelessness. Depressed children may experience changes in their mood and behaviour, and here feelings of anger or acting out may mask an underlying depression. It's important to recognize these signs and seek appropriate support and treatment for the child.

Over time, children as well as adults may find that the death of a loved one changes their values, even if it's not immediately recognized as a reaction. They may become more aware of what they believe truly matters in life, learn to appreciate others more, and strengthen their bonds with important people. They may also develop strength and insight into how to support others during times of crisis (Oltjenbruns, 1991).

Children who have experienced a loss may take on new roles in the family and become caregivers for their parents or siblings. This can bring a sense of purpose and pride, and they may offer support and comfort by saying things like, 'We'll get through this together.'

> Emma, aged 9, supported her mother after her father died in an accident, saying: 'We'll be fine, the three of us' (Emma, mother and little brother). After her father's death, Emma began to call her mother very often to check that she was okay.

However, it's important to watch out for situations where children take on too much responsibility and neglect their own needs, especially if the surviving parent is struggling to cope. While it's important not to discourage children from helping out after a loss, it's important for adults to be aware of the child's emotional and social needs, and to ensure that they are still able to maintain a healthy balance of responsibilities and activities, such as school and socializing with friends.

Grief over time

As we said at the start of this chapter, children's reactions to death vary widely. While some get their lives back to normal relatively quickly, others experience reactions that last a very long time. Difficult experiences in life may trigger new reactions or new real-izations. As children age, they may develop a deeper understand-ing of the loss, leading to a re-evaluation of what happened and a renewed period of longing. Triggers can include events like school graduations where the deceased is absent, encountering someone who resembles the deceased, hearing music that was played at the funeral, or visiting the grave site. These triggers can cause a resur-gence of grief and other reactions months or years after the death, which others may struggle to understand. In Chapter 6 (Compli-cated Grief Processes), we discuss signs that a child's reactions require professional assistance.

Conclusion

In this chapter, we have described some of the many and varied grief reactions children may experience in the aftermath of the loss of a parent, sibling, or other loved one. Responses vary based on the type of loss, the child's age and personality, and the available community support. There are no right or wrong ways to grieve, and no singular 'normal' response to loss. By referring to 'normal grief reactions', we imply that the reactions discussed in this chapter do not necessarily require psychological therapy, and can instead be managed in the immediate environment with the help of family, school, and com-munity resources, such as conversation-based grief groups. It is only when you find that the child's responses become distressing and threaten their long-term well-being and health, or they appear to be persistent or increasing in intensity, that grief should be considered problematic and require therapeutic intervention.

Chapter 2

Meeting Children in Grief

'Teachers should try to put themselves in our place. They should just think that we really want to have a say. It's about us, so why shouldn't we have a say?' *Aoife, aged 12*

One piece of advice commonly given to new educators is that, while adults and children are equal in worth, adults hold a greater responsibility as authorities. For although we have equal worth, as adults we have a greater responsibility to bear. This applies to parents, friends, and family, and not least to those of us who have to meet children in a professional context as teachers, health professionals, or therapists. As professionals, we must ensure that children thrive and develop, and as parents, we have an additional responsibility to ensure that they have food and shelter. It is therefore natural for most adults to take the lead when children experience difficult situations in life.

In our practice, we have often encountered adults who – in the best sense – try to protect children in crisis by making as many decisions for them as possible. The reason lies in a historical understanding that adults know best, but also in a compassionate belief that children in a difficult period should not have to deal with more than is necessary. The idea of including children's perspectives in research and studies of child welfare is thus new and not something that was seen much of 20 years ago. For the same reason, expert literature and guidelines on children's grief are almost always based on adults' understanding of it. Similarly, adult perspectives on the help that grieving children need continue to dominate the field.

Many of you reading this book are parents or carers in the child's family. You will often be directly affected yourself, because you have lost a partner, a child, a grandchild, or another person close to you. In this context, it is important to know that you yourself may be deeply affected and spend a lot of energy dealing with the loss, and your parenting or caring skills can be weakened. One of the most important things you can do over time to be there for a child is to give yourself time to take in the loss and process what has happened, and to think from a long-term perspective. While it may be tempting in the short term to protect your child from emotional pain, it may be unwise in the long run.

Your role in relation to the child will determine how much you can do for the child. As a teacher, you are in a position to help the child in a different way than if you are their football coach. What you can say or do depends on how well you know them. If you yourself have experienced a painful loss in your life, it is important that you are clear about this so that your own loss and reactions do not complicate your contact with the child.

In this chapter, we describe what is important in meeting children in grief. We have tried to understand what kind of help the children themselves want and what is most important to them. When you have read the chapter, we hope that you will have an understanding of what constitutes 'good adult help' and what support children themselves say that they would like. An important foundation for all support is to see the child as an expert on their own grief.

Good adult support

If you ask professionals who work with children what support or help children need, most will quickly come up with some general guidelines. However, there is often a big difference between what adults and children themselves define as good help.

So what is good help? Do children want adults to take control and look after them following a loss? Or do they want adults to involve them? Is there a difference in the support children want from parents, educators, and teachers? The answers to these questions are many and are further complicated by the fact that every child's story is unique, which undeniably leads to individual needs. There is therefore no single right answer.

Despite the unique and individual nature of children's grief reactions, there are several commonalities. Few children desire to have their grief silenced or hidden away, whether within the family or in their interactions with professionals. Most children do not want parents or caregivers to withhold the truth or obscure the gravity of a situation, leaving them to grieve alone. Our experience suggests that children prefer to be involved in conversations and decision-making processes regarding the support measures put in place to help them. Simultaneously, they also wish to retain the ability to decline interventions that they do not find meaningful or enjoyable. Involvement provides children with a sense of security by allowing them to anticipate what will happen and reducing the likelihood of encountering situations that make them uncomfortable. While the level of a child's participation may vary based on their personality, developmental stage, and age, even those who lack decision-making authority benefit from understanding what will occur. Therefore, it is important for responsible adults to be transparent with children. In the following section, we offer 14 tips for adults that serve as a foundation for how we believe parents and professionals can engage with grieving children. These recommendations reflect core principles that guide our approach to supporting children through the grieving process.

Tip 1: Respect the child's wishes

Despite the fact that children typically desire support and collaboration in navigating their grief, they may also experience conflicting feelings about the type of support they wish to receive. On the one hand, children want to be met by adults who understand and are interested in their life situation. On the other hand, they are afraid of appearing different, especially in adolescence. As an adult, it is natural to want to take away the pain that the children you meet are experiencing in the difficult situation they are facing. Unfortunately, this is not always possible when children experience life-threatening illness and death. We must therefore prepare ourselves for the fact that children do not always leave us feeling better after a difficult conversation. Sometimes they are just as upset after we have spoken to them as they were before we met. That doesn't mean you've done anything wrong. It means you've shared something difficult with them. It's important that you dare to accept the pain the children are feeling – and that it can be shared safely.

Some children want you to make it clear that you are there for them. They want to hear you say it, or for your gaze to tell them that you see them. This is especially true for children of pre-school age, while youngsters may want the opposite: for you to pay no extra attention to them, at least not in front of others. Most want something in between – they want to know you're thinking about them, but not too visibly. So you need to take advantage of situations where others may be preoccupied with their own tasks to let them know more discreetly that you are thinking about them, that they are in a special situation, and that you are there for them if they want to talk or you can be helpful in some other way. The best way to ensure that you tread carefully enough is to talk to children about how they want contact before they return to school, sports clubs, or similar. Remember too that as time goes on, a child's wishes may change, so you need to consult with them to see if they would like a different approach over time. If a child reacts with strong feelings, these are not usually dangerous, and you can acknowledge them with a look and by putting into words what you are experiencing. But be careful about interpreting what you think they are feeling or thinking. You can say, 'I can see that this is difficult for you, but I don't really know how you are experiencing it. Can you tell me a bit about it so I can understand better?' In such a situation, you may also be surprised that the child's reaction was not due to grief, as you might have thought.

Tip 2: Don't underestimate children's experiences

We are often surprised by how little adults have perceived of what children experienced in the event of a death – especially if the child was present at the time of death. It is natural that all attention is focused on the deceased or the person delivering the message of death, and therefore what children experience (see, hear, perceive, etc.) often goes under the radar. It can be difficult for adults to know what the children have understood, how intense the experience has been for them, and how much it resonates with them afterwards. Although we are talking here about the concrete experience, sometimes the children's thoughts and feelings can also be misjudged. We are not mind readers, and as children often hide their reactions to protect adults, it is easy to underestimate how much the situation affects them. That's why we need to tell them that they don't need to protect us, and be open to signals and signs of how the death is affecting them. There is nothing to stop us asking what the worst thing is that has happened, but it is also easy to read too much into children's reactions or lack of them. It can be logical to assume that children are not coping well if they don't talk much about the death. However, it's crucial to consider how they are functioning in other areas of their life, such as their social interactions and school performance. It's also important to keep in mind that children may have a rich inner world of thoughts and emotions that they may not express openly.

Tip 3: Be aware that children easily pick up on adult cues

From an early age, children are sensitive to how adults around them act and react. They interpret moods and can easily become anxious when they do not understand adult reactions. Deaths in the family affect both adults and children, and bereavement and longing create a new atmosphere in the home that children need to understand. They may be frightened by parental crying, and by irritation and anger, and feel that the absence of the usual adult attention is unsettling. At the same time, it is not uncommon for children, both in the run-up to and after a death, to overhear conversations that their parents did not intend them to hear. This can create a breeding ground for fragmented knowledge, where children know only some of the truth, not all of it. If they find they cannot share their knowledge with adults because the truth is hidden from them, this creates opportunities for filling in the gaps with fantasies and fears.

> 'We overheard Maya, aged four, saying to Ken, aged two, "You just have to know that two or three days after she's had chemo, she's in bed and it's bad, so we have to be quiet." She picked that up from conversations we had with family and friends. It was an eye-opener for us, and led up to adopt another approach. She shouldn't hear it that way and then create her own ideas. What she needs to know, she needs to hear directly from us.' *Father of Maya and Ken*

When children are involved, their questions or reactions can easily affect adults. Children may notice that certain questions or topics cause tears, silence, or withdrawal from adults, and they may become hesitant to bring up these subjects again. It's natural for children to want to protect adults from pain and they may avoid asking or talking about something that they believe will upset their parents. While it's important for parents to be open about their reactions to grief, it's also important to put those reactions into words so that children can understand them and be less afraid. Parents should explain to their children that adults' grief is different from children's grief.

Adults' responses to difficult situations often appear more consistent than those of children; they may be sad in longer periods without much variation. As one child aptly put it, 'We have so much else to think about.' However, it is important to recognize how easily children can misinterpret or misunderstand adults' reactions, as the following example illustrates:

> A 13-year-old who lost her mother in an accident got a new puppy a few weeks later. When she showed the dog to some friends, her father saw her smile for the first time after her mother's death. It made him cry. When he told her about it, the girl spontaneously said: 'Is that why you were crying? I thought it was something I said.'

Tip 4: Make time for the child

As an adult, you have many responsibilities to juggle. Even without having to support a child dealing with a life-threatening illness or loss, finding enough time can be a challenge. However, it is good for children to feel heard and supported by adults who make time for them. It takes a lot of courage for children to open up and talk about difficult experiences, and if they feel brushed aside or ignored, they are unlikely to ask again. Delaying the conversation can be interpreted as a lack of interest or priority, leading to a breakdown of trust. Therefore, we encourage you to seize the opportunity to discuss difficult topics when they arise. These conversations are often the most authentic and meaningful, and they show the child that you are there for them when they need you. Building this trust increases the chances of future conversations and can be a key foundation for ongoing support.

If you are unable to have the conversation with the child when they approach you, it's crucial not to dismiss their need to talk and delay the conversation indefinitely. Instead, acknowledge their approach and express your appreciation for their willingness to share. Let them know that discussing their concerns is important and set a specific time to have the conversation as soon as possible, at a time that works for both of you. As a parent, it's essential to be aware that children may prefer to talk at bedtime or during car rides when eye contact is not as direct. While this may not be the most convenient time for you, it's important to follow through and honour the arranged time for the conversation.

Tip 5: Remember to be open and direct in communications with children

All our experience tells us that we can talk directly to children about death. You shouldn't use paraphrases like 'now that your dad is no longer with us' or other attempts to soften the loss. Be direct and honest in your communication. If it is suicide, use the word 'suicide', and if it is murder, say 'murder'. Don't say you understand; instead say that you can imagine it's hard, and you can't know how they feel because you haven't experienced anything like it yourself. And even if you have experienced the same thing, you still can't know exactly how it is for them. In that case, you can tell the child. If you don't know exactly what happened, ask if they can tell you or if you should ask about it – and then they can answer.

> When a young girl entered the psychologist's office, she immediately said, 'If you ask me to tell, I'll leave.' The psychologist found her statement unusual and asked her about it. The girl explained that after her friend's suicide, a doctor had asked her to 'start telling her story' without offering any other options. When the girl asked if he could ask her questions instead, he replied, 'That's not how we do it here.' Despite her initial reluctance, the psychologist engaged the girl in conversation, but she didn't have to take the lead.

If you are having a conversation with a child who has lost a loved one, you may briefly bring up painful topics because the child is already thinking a lot about these. You can ask how they were told, what they saw if they were there, what it's like to be at home now without the deceased, and so on. If the child is very reluctant to talk and tries to push away what has happened, then you should proceed gently. You can talk about the fact that it will almost always be difficult if children want to avoid anything that reminds them of the deceased, be it conversations about things, situations, or places. Explain that it is important to talk about what has happened and the pain it brings, but not too much at once. These children cannot handle long conversations about loss and longing, so you have to be prepared for short visits to themes of grief. In Chapter 11 (Therapy with Children), we discuss how to proceed in therapy when grief has taken hold in this way.

Tip 6: Accept what children tell you and confirm what they experience

It is a difficult art to confirm children in their grief, especially if they say little. But then you have to risk being wrong. For example, 'I guess you are afraid that something will happen to your mother too' takes into account that children who lose parents are often afraid that something will happen to the other parent as well. Many will nod or say yes, and you can continue the conversation and ask what they are thinking. Others may deny it, but you can sense that they are not being completely honest and you may say, 'That's normal, and if you should experience it, please know that there are many children and adults who think like that. It happened once, so why can't it happen again? But remember, it's very rare for this kind of death to happen. If you are troubled by these thoughts a lot, there are methods you can learn that can help you.' (See Chapter 7, Coping with Loss.)

You can follow up and confirm what the children tell you and help them to get more form, structure, language, and benefits out of the thoughts, impressions, and reactions they experience. By confirming their feelings and helping them find appropriate words and perhaps recognize the feelings better, you are expanding their ways of regulating emotions with words.

In conversations with children, adults can help children put their experiences into words by using open-ended questions such as, 'Can you say more about this?' or, 'You said you think about her most after you go to bed. Can you tell me what you think about then?' You can also start with some opening words that show you understand their situation: 'Other children who have lost a parent have told you that they feel guilty because they were not with their mum/dad more when she/he was ill, or because they said something they were sorry for. Is this something you think about?'

Tip 7: Follow up on what they say – or be one step ahead

In conversations with children, you need to both follow up and be ahead. If children start a conversation, follow it up: 'Have you been angry with her since you said this?' If a child describes an aspect of grief, for example, 'Dad liked spaghetti too', this can be followed up with: 'I think you miss him when you eat something he liked?' This means you are both following up and affirming.

But we also need to be up front, not least because children have so little experience with what grief is. We need to use our experience to guide children: 'It is not uncommon for us to feel as if the person who has died is with us. Sometimes it gets a little scary if it feels as if the person is in the room, but that's how it is when you miss someone a lot.' Of course, we can't talk about what's normal all the time, but when we share our experience in situations where we sense a child is preoccupied with the person who has died, we help to broaden their understanding of what they are experiencing.

If a child is crying or a young person is upset, adults who put this into words or give simple advice on what they can do to endure or quell the grief will develop their ability to regulate emotions. This could be setting aside a fixed time to approach the loss and otherwise diverting attention, writing down what they are experiencing, being in contact with others, and so on. In particular, parents or the remaining parent have a very important role in teaching children different strategies for emotion regulation. Here we adults are role models, where children observe what we do, but we can also tell them about what we ourselves do to cope with difficult feelings and thoughts.

For example, following up as a parent can mean noticing what the child is asking about or how they are feeling, and addressing this later: 'I was thinking about our chat last night and wanted to ask if you're feeling extra sad now because we're getting close to the day when they passed away. I've been feeling really sad too, and it's not a good feeling. But it's nice that we have each other because we can help make each other feel better.'

Tip 8: Remember your role as a professional

'Showing emotion depends on whether it's a teacher you have a personal relationship with. Because it would just seem weird, I think, if a teacher I didn't have a special relationship with came and said, "How sad for you, Anna." Then I think I would have just felt a bit weird, too.' *Anna, aged 12*

Children want to talk to adults who are present and compassionate, but they also want such adults to fulfil their professional role. If a child talks with an adult who is very upset and cries a lot, it can be difficult to find room for their own grief. Children are intuitive and you may end up in a situation where the child feels that it is more important to comfort and protect you than to show their own feelings. A 15-year-old girl who had lost an alcoholic father said that shortly after the loss she ended up comforting a teacher who was crying and telling her about her own childhood with a similar experience. The roles were reversed, and the girl found the situation extremely uncomfortable. Such situations not only make the child feel awkward in the moment but also give them the impression that the adult cannot handle the situation and is therefore not someone they can talk to about difficult things.

It is important to remember that being a professional does not mean you cannot show emotion or offer comfort to a grieving child. If you have previously shown affection or given hugs to the child, it is appropriate to continue doing so during difficult times. However, if you have not done so before, it may seem unusual to suddenly start. The same applies to showing emotion. If the child is accustomed to you expressing emotion, it is appropriate to do so during the conversation. The same basic rule applies if you are upset or clearly affected by a discussion: tell the child why. This will help you regain control of the conversation and show that you understand the emotions involved in the child's situation and that it's okay to be upset. Emotions cannot be taken out of the situation – neither yours nor the child's. The most important basic rule, however, is that your feelings should not outweigh the child's.

Tip 9: Ask the child for advice

Children (especially older ones) want to have the opportunity to comment on what is being done to support them. First, it ensures that the support provided is aligned with their specific needs. Second, it is not recommended to impose support on children that they are not ready for or do not want. Therefore, it is important to have a respectful and inclusive approach to children in bereavement work. As a parent, if you feel that your child could benefit from seeing a psychologist, it is essential to explain why and what such help means. Forcing a child to see a professional may lead to an unmotivated child who is more challenging to help.

It is not always easy to know which support measures are most appropriate. We recommend that when doubts arise, you take the child concerned into account. Consider the child as an 'expert' on their own grief. If you disagree with the child's decision, it is often better to explain why and find a compromise together than to force through something the child is against from the start. This approach is doomed to fail. If, on the other hand, a mutually respectful and inclusive working environment is created, it will be easier for a child to share dilemmas and challenges. Compromise can also be helpful here, so, for example, if the child does not want to see a psychologist, they can give them a chance before deciding whether to continue. Occasionally, the situation may require time too, and for help to be offered at a later stage. Cooperation of this kind creates the basis for the most effective and best possible support.

Tip 10: Be discreet

'I don't like being constantly greeted with "How are you today?" It constantly reminds me of what I've lost.' *Lisa, aged 16*

Timing is important when talking to children about difficult topics. It's best to avoid interrupting them during moments of joy or in public settings where they might feel embarrassed or exposed. For example, it's not appropriate to approach a child while they're laughing with friends to ask how they're coping with grief. Similarly, singling out a child who has experienced a loss in front of their peers can be uncomfortable and hurtful. Instead, choose a private moment when the child feels comfortable and secure, and approach the topic with sensitivity and respect.

In both cases above, it is positive that the adult tries to be caring, but illness and loss are experienced by many as very private and it may lead to feelings of vulnerability. Children therefore rarely want grief to be discussed without being prepared for it and agreeing to it. They want the support and help to be discreet. It is about seizing the opportunity when it arises. Such spontaneous conversations often work much better than sitting across from each other with a table between. If you are unsure about how the child specifically wants contact to take place, you can ask them about their wishes and needs. This way you can make sure that the support you give is on the child's terms.

Tip 11: Establish special rules with the child

'These rules were one of the first things I was told. It was really nice. You just knew what the rules were.' *Christine, aged 12, about school*

Supporting a child through the life-threatening illness or death of a loved one is unfamiliar to most of us. Likewise, it is also a new and unfamiliar world for the grieving child to navigate. Here the child must go through a learning process, learning to cope with their own grief reactions and the new life circumstances that the loss has brought. It is therefore natural that the grieving child will struggle for a long time to learn to live with their grief.

It is also only natural that unforeseen and difficult thoughts may suddenly intrude in everyday life. Without being prepared for this to happen, or knowing specifically what is happening, a child may find themselves in difficult situations where they are unsure of what the right thing to do is. Whether at school or at an after-school activity, should the child leave the lesson or activity if they become upset? Should the child ask the adults for permission or just leave? Is it better to stay in the situation and pretend nothing is happening, even if the child feels uncomfortable? In some cases, these concerns become so serious that the child breaks down and cries, and leaves the class or the sports field. This creates an unnecessary situation that frightens both adults and other children and may require a subsequent explanation. Such situations are also experienced as very unpleasant by the grieving child. Therefore, agree on 'rules' with the child for such situations.

Tip 12: Involve children in rituals and commemorations, but with care

'Personally, I would not raise the flag at half-mast, as was done in school. It would be a bit too much for the other children to be 'involved like that. I think it would have been better if, for example, they had made a little card or written a personal greeting.' *Ella, aged 14*

As described earlier, life-threatening illness and death put children in an unfamiliar situation. Suddenly they face a series of challenges they have no experience of. And at the same time, they find that their family has fewer resources to support them. In the vast majority of cases, this creates uncertainty for a child about what the future will look like.

Children need to be involved in family rituals. They need to be well prepared, they need good adult support through the rituals, and they need to be followed up afterwards. We write about this in Chapter 8 (Grief in the Family). But outside the family it is also natural to mark deaths that affect the community, for example if a pupil or teacher dies. These can be ritual acts such as flying the flag at half-mast or singing a special song. The ideas and celebrations can be positive, but it is important that siblings of a deceased pupil, for example, do not feel singled out.

When a child's life has been drastically changed by a difficult situation, it can be uncomfortable for them to deal with the attention and opinions of others. However, it's still important to acknowledge and mark the situation in some way. It's essential to consider the child's perspective and be aware of any worries that may arise. Before taking any action, it's best to talk to the child and ask for their input and preferences. In our experience, young children may be more willing to participate in rituals or commemorations, whereas teenagers often prefer to avoid standing out.

Tip 13: Remember that grief lasts over time

'You will miss the person for the rest of your life, so why should you only be sad for a short period of your life? I can still be sad without breaking down and crying. I am still sad and think about the person, but there can also be periods when I feel good and think about it in a good way. It varies.' *Anna, aged 15*

Many children feel that the loss will soon be forgotten by their circle of friends when everyday life returns. As a result, they often feel alone with their grief and find that while they may miss someone so much it hurts, the world just goes on. At the same time, many children find that others do not handle it well when they mention the loss. This can leave them feeling that their loss is uncomfortable for others to talk about and that it is therefore best to avoid bringing it up.

On the other hand, children may also be very surprised and frightened if grief suddenly returns in a new and strengthened form, and they may think that this is a very abnormal reaction. However, modern grief theory such as the dual process model of bereavement (Stroebe & Schut, 1999) has described how it is quite normal for grief to return in different ways and at different strengths at different periods of our lives. For children in particular, it is natural for grief to return as they understand new aspects of themselves and thereby also comprehend the meaning of their loss in new ways. This can be when Mum is missing for their confirmation, Christmas Eve, or an important sports match when everyone else has their parents with them. Children say that difficult situations usually occur when the class gets new teachers or they change schools, where the loss is not known. Then, for example, topics like serious illness or death can be brought up without them being prepared for it. It is therefore important that staff at a new school are informed of the child's situation.

As a support person, it is essential to be aware that a child may repeatedly return to the loss during your contact with them, and you can take the opportunity to talk to them, validate their thoughts, and reminisce together. These conversations strengthen your relationship and let the child know that they are not alone in remembering the loss, even if it happened years ago.

Such conversations may be all that is needed, and new support measures may not be necessary unless you are concerned about the child's general well-being.

Tip 14: Support the child in maintaining friendships

'It's important that your friends still remember you as who you are, and not think of you as someone who has changed and who is not the same person.' *Theis, aged 11*

When children experience life-threatening illness or death, their family and daily lives change suddenly and dramatically. A home that was previously safe and stable can suddenly become unsafe and changed. It is natural and advisable that many children may want to return to previous activities, such as school, as soon as possible because they represent something normal and stable in their lives. But children's lives have not only changed at home – grief follows them to school and changes the situation there too. On the first day back, children meet adults who offer condolences and classmates who rarely know how to cope with the loss. What to say? Is it best to pretend nothing happened? At the same time, grief and worry are rarely things that can be left at home, and the sadness and sense of loss follow the grieving children wherever they go.

One of the biggest challenges for grieving children is that they often feel different when they return to school and extracurricular activities. Life is no longer the same as before and it can be difficult to be as happy and cheerful as their classmates and friends. Situations can quickly arise where neither peers nor a bereaved child dare mention the loss for fear of upsetting each other. Unfortunately, this often leads to the grieving pupil feeling alone and isolated. In the worst-case scenario, this lack of understanding develops into bullying. This can particularly be the case among younger children who do not yet understand what it is like to live with a life-threatening illness or death in the family.

It is therefore desirable for the class teacher, for example, to help create a framework for talking about what has happened. If this is done well, it can ensure that peers become an important support rather than a burden for the bereaved child. Here, teachers can arrange for young people to have a conversation together about how to be a good friend, and can convey how the bereaved person would like others to relate to them. Always remember to inform the person concerned of what is going to happen before you start any support measures. This will make the child or young person feel involved and ensure that it does not come as an unpleasant surprise. We have written more about how friends can be supportive in Chapter 9, Grief and Relationships.

Conclusion

The advice provided in this chapter is informed by both experience and studies, offering general guidance for supporting grieving children. However, it's important to acknowledge that each child's needs are unique, as their grief is influenced by various factors such as personality, age, background, social resources, and the type of loss. Providing support to a grieving child can be complicated due to these individualized needs. It's important to seek feedback from the child about how they are feeling and what they need, as the best support is often collaboratively determined.

Chapter 3

Development and Children's Grief

Introduction

Just a few decades ago, professionals doubted whether children were capable of experiencing grief at all, assuming that they lacked the mental tools to conceptualize death and its consequences, like adults. Although this notion is now thankfully behind us, adults may still believe that children do not understand when difficult information needs to be communicated to them. Therefore, it is important to describe what children comprehend and feel, drawing not only from theories but also from our experiences working with bereaved children. Theories are only valid until reality shows us otherwise.

Childhood spans from 0 to 18 years, and it follows that children's experiences of grief can vary greatly. In this chapter, we will illustrate how children's understanding of death and their grieving process evolve with age and development, and how loss can impact their further growth. Our goal is to provide you with a better understanding of the differences between losing someone as a toddler and losing someone as a teenager. We will also examine the differences and similarities in the way boys and girls respond to loss.

Children's understanding of death at different ages

Children's conceptual understanding develops gradually through childhood. In the first years of life, the brain is constantly making new neural connections, initially at an almost unimaginable pace. Children gain new experiences through their activities and through interactions with others in the family, in nurseries, and at school. They are constantly absorbing new experiences, which they synthesize with what they have experienced before; they undergo motor and mental development, and they continue to form changing maps of the world of which they are a part. They create and reshape their concepts based on experience in close interaction with the environment. Developing an understanding of death is not a passive process. A child is constantly testing their understanding by interaction with the world around them. Therefore, it is understandable that the development of understanding of death takes place at different rates in different children, while the development or sequence of what they understand is usually similar. Maturation reflects children's experience, but also the fact that experience is filtered through their growing capacity to think more complex thoughts as they age and they gain increased conceptual understanding.

Young children (0–5 years old)

Usually, children's maturation and conceptual development do not allow children under six to have a well-developed understanding of what life is and how the body and body parts work. They also do not understand that death is permanent and that someone is gone 'forever'. Young children will often believe that the deceased will return – that death is something from which one can return. We see this when children say things like:

- 'She'll be back in a fortnight, won't she?'

- 'When he comes, we'll play hide and seek.'

Death to them is reversible, and they do not understand that the body no longer 'works':

- 'Who's going to cut her hair now?'

- 'Can she hear anything through all that dirt?'

Nor do they understand that death will happen to everyone, that it is universal:

- 'Can little boys die too?'

When we explain things to young children, we have to be concrete, because they don't have the prerequisites to understand the abstract. If we tell them that someone is with Jesus, it is not easy for them to understand that they are also buried in the ground. We can see how they become confused:

- 'Where can we take the bus to Jesus?'

Our clear advice is that it is best to avoid abstract explanations. The same applies to paraphrases, which children can take very literally. Saying that the deceased is going on a long journey can create anxiety about travelling, or a desire to go where the deceased is. In the past, older people were often said to fall asleep when they died. This is not so common now, but children still hear this and watch adults when they sleep on the couch, or they themselves become afraid to sleep. Irene, aged 4, would wake her mother if she lay down for a nap on the sofa. She had heard the adults talking about her grandmother who had fallen asleep (see also Chapter 4, The Impact of Loss on Children's Lives). 'Passing away' can be misunderstood in the same way.

When children show through their questions that they don't understand the finality of death, for example by asking, 'When will Dad be back?', the honest answer is 'He won't, but do you think about him much?' Then you can explain that when you are dead, you don't breathe anymore, your hair doesn't grow, and so on.

Although young children may not have a fully developed concept of death, they can still have strong reactions to it. Children react to separation and express their grief, for example by seeking out places where they expect to find the deceased; even children under the age of two may do this.

> Noah, who was only one-and-a-half years old, had a sister who passed away in her cradle. In the initial days following her death, he would approach her cradle and questioningly utter, 'Ba?' Her bed was eventually put away, but several months later, it was brought back out for a visiting child. At that moment, Noah went up to the cradle, peeked inside, and asked 'Ba?' once again.

However, because of their lack of experience, young children can easily get the wrong idea about what can cause death. For example, they may say things like, 'If you hadn't gone to the hospital, the baby wouldn't be dead.'

Children need explanations that are adapted to their age or maturity level so that they can gradually develop their understanding as they learn. Some explore in concrete terms what death means. During the viewing of a body, they may stick a finger up the nose to see what is happening, or lightly touch the eyelids of the deceased. Others may bury a dead wasp and then dig it up again later to see what has happened to it.

Young children's concept of time is often circular: they get up, eat, go to nursery, come home, go back to bed – and so the days move forward. They therefore also have a circular concept of time. Their lives repeat themselves. So it's not surprising that they imagine that we live first, then die, then live again.

Children with a lack of experience can easily perceive themselves as the centre of things and they may believe that their thoughts, feelings, desires, and actions can be the cause of what happens to themselves or others. They may believe that the deceased can be recalled if one so wishes. But more often and more problematically, they can believe that they are to blame for a death.

Young children's lack of understanding of what death is and of the long-term significance of death can mean that they react little to the first news of what has happened. Parents report that just after being told that a parent or a sibling has died, their child may say: 'Can I go and play now?' Later that day, they may come and ask: 'When is he coming home?' No wonder it was long thought that young children could not grieve.

> 'We thought there would be a reaction from him. There was nothing. He mentioned his dad once in a while, like, "When my dad comes down from heaven, we're going to the swimming pool." But then nothing happened, he wasn't angry or upset.'
> *Social educator*

Young children's imagination can be expressed through play activities. Let's take some examples. An educator told us how all the children in the nursery school were busy rolling sand pancakes after a parent had been run over and killed. They wanted to see what it looked like when someone 'went flat as a pancake'. Another educator found that all the nursery school children were busy playing funeral, as a few of them had attended a funeral of a parent. They mostly disagreed about how many of them could be priests. Although such a game can seem macabre in many ways, it is also a way for children to process what they have experienced. Often what is uncomfortable for the children is not the game, but if an obviously shocked adult suddenly stops it. This just teaches children that death is something to be afraid of and not something to talk about.

Pre-school children also have a weaker degree of emotional differentiation than older children, and they have less experience regulating or dampening their emotions (Widen & Russell, 2010). They may say they are 'very, very, very sorry', using the word 'very' repeatedly to describe an emotion rather than using a new expression.

If young children see parents being sad, they may be sad themselves. They respond to their parents' 'mood' and may seek them out for companionship or comfort. They may demand more attention, becoming angry or clingy. They may also express their distress by saying that their stomach hurts.

Although the understanding of death among children is limited by their age and maturity, a concrete encounter with death in the family can accelerate their understanding and give them a more mature perspective than their peers.

> Gordon, aged four-and-a-half, lost his best friend in an accident. Before he saw his friend in the coffin, he showed his lack of understanding of the finality of death by saying, 'In 14 days, when the summer holidays are over, he'll be back.' On the way home, he expressed a more mature understanding: 'Now we can never go swimming together again. Now we can never hammer wood again.'

Concrete memories are usually well received by young children. For example, a small table could be set up with a picture of the deceased, where they can light a candle when they miss the person, or a picture could be hung in the child's wardrobe. Activities can also include a memory box with things and pictures that the child can take out when needed. However, we always recommend that professionals ask whether the child and the family think it is a good idea before starting such activities.

As an adult, you play an important role for the child at this age because young children prefer to be comforted and helped by an adult rather than by their friends. This means that you, as a professional, will often have more contact with a grieving young child than at later ages, and that they will need more of your help to understand and get through the grief.

Children aged five to ten years

Between the ages of five and ten, children gradually develop a greater understanding that death is irreversible and that all life functions cease: 'When you're dead, you're dead.' This is linked to a better understanding of what the different organs of the body are used for, and how they combine to allow a person to live. Around the age of six, children will have developed a more psychological understanding of what life is. While young children may think that a heart exists to love someone, the lungs to talk and the stomach to eat, children close to or of school age will understand that the body and the main organs all have a common goal: to sustain 'life' (Slaughter, 2005). Once this more complex understanding of the body and its organs is developed, the basis is in place for a better understanding of what happens if organs fail or are destroyed.

Around the age of seven, children seem to have a better understanding that death is inevitable and universal, and that the deceased is not coming back. However, they may still often have difficulty understanding that death as something that can happen to them. Like younger children, they are still concrete in their thoughts and need concrete expressions (rituals, pictures, burial place, etc.) to support them in their grieving process. Their understanding of the cause is also concrete. They can understand death both as a result of external events, such as accidents and violence, and as caused by internal processes, such as illness and old age. However, they may not always link the cause of death to actual processes – for example, that a father died because his liver was damaged by too much alcohol.

At this age, children think less egocentrically and are better able to understand the perspective of others and thus have greater compassion for those who have lost siblings or parents, and for their own family members who are grieving. Although children can comfort and show care for others even before the age of two and also have the ability to show compassion (empathy), this is more pronounced as they get older. Children aged five to ten understand more about the cause and effect behind events, and they may be preoccupied with the unfairness of things happening – that bad things happen to good people: 'It wasn't fair for it to happen to her, she was always so nice.' Children also master these concepts by understanding and 'getting' the facts about what happened. The older children become, the more they will build their understanding by understanding details of the incident themselves (e.g., asking questions, searching the web).

Already by the age of five, but more clearly after that, there seems to be a certain shift in children's willingness to show their feelings. In particular, boys may begin to hide their feelings as learning takes place in the friendship group and through the influence of adult attitudes. Many parents find that children close off their grief and are unwilling to talk about what has happened, or at least do not want further conversations about the death. (See also Chapter 6, Complicated Grief Processes, on the balance between approaching their loss or moving away from it.)

Children over ten years

As children reach the age of ten, their ideas about death begin to take on a more abstract form and they gain a deeper understanding of the long-term implications of death. They may reflect more on topics such as justice, injustice, fate, and the supernatural. The combination of biological, psychological, and social changes that occur during adolescence can trigger strong emotional responses to death. Although adolescents are capable of considering death as an abstract concept, the realization that it is a universal and inevitable part of life also means that it becomes more personal and can have an impact on them. As a result, they may feel the need to keep thoughts of death at a distance.

In adolescence, the ability to think hypothetically develops, allowing young people to assess different aspects of an event, including how it could have been avoided. They draw parallels more

easily and are able to assess inconsistencies in the facts they learn
more critically. They can question what they are told if it does not
match what they hear adults talking about, or other information
they find, for example on the internet. They may also be very critical
of their own actions in relation to the death. After adolescence, their
concepts of death might develop as a result of the deaths of peers
and friends, through suicide, illness, or accidents. They additionally
become able to reflect on deeper issues and more existential aspects
of death and life.

> George, aged 15, lost his elder brother in an accident. He was very
> sad for a long time, not least about the many things he knew his
> big brother would never experience, including watching his son
> grow up. His ability to see the future made him reflect on what his
> brother was missing and what he would never experience with him.
> He spent time thinking about why this should happen to him and
> his brother, and why it should happen to someone as gentle and
> good as his brother. He also spoke of how deeply he felt the loss of
> a role model who had always been there for him. He understood
> that this loss would cast shadows into the rest of his life.

Around the age of 12, fitting in becomes increasingly important
for children. This is a dilemma for most teenagers, but for those
bereaved, the death of a loved one can be concrete proof of being
different and understanding the world in a different way. Many
bereaved children in this age group feel that they do not fit in
because the loss has in many ways taken away the innocence their
friends possess. Many are also afraid of getting too much attention
during this time. They do not want schools to mark their loss or
to organize memorial services to which their friends are invited, as
this draws too much attention and emphasizes that they are now
different. At the same time, young people may also have a strong
desire to share the difficult experience at an age when help from
friends is often seen as more important than support from adults.

It can be difficult for young people to navigate between the need to feel like everyone else and wanting to be able to share the difficult life experience with their friends. This is where adults can help to create a good framework for talking about death in a group of friends (see more on this in Chapter 10, Navigating Grief in the Classroom). Grief groups where young people can share their experiences with others in the same situation may also be an appropriate approach. However, we should not forget that at the same time young people may find it really nice to have a break from grief and just be with their friends – perhaps especially if these are friends with whom they can also share their grief and longing at other times, outside school.

Although our understanding of how children comprehend death across different cultures is limited, research suggests that there are no significant differences in a child's understanding of death across continents (Cuddy-Casey & Orvaschel, 1997). However, there are notable variations across cultures in how openly and directly children are informed about a death and its cause, and the extent to which they are involved in the farewell and funeral processes. Work with children in various parts of the world during times of war and disaster has shown a gradual shift towards more open and direct communication with children about serious issues across different cultures.

How does loss affect children's development?

Although research has explored how children respond to the loss of parents and siblings, there is still limited knowledge about how it affects their cognitive and emotional development. While it is evident that such losses impact academic performance and emotional well-being in adulthood, there is insufficient understanding of how and when such difficulties arise in childhood (see Chapter 4, The Impact of Loss on Children's Lives).

Studies reveal that adults who lost parents during childhood find it challenging to articulate their emotions, which may affect their ability to form relationships later in life (Calderon *et al.*, 2019). In our clinical practice, we've seen adults who have experienced the loss of a loved one during childhood reach out to address feelings of emotional detachment. The ability to regulate emotions develops in childhood through interactions with parents, who act as role models, teaching children how to manage inner turmoil and gradually develop the skill to suppress overwhelming emotions. Other adults, such as teachers and friends, also contribute to this development over time.

When children lose parents or siblings, not only do they lose a role model; they may also have a remaining parent who is struggling with their own grief reactions, making them emotionally unavailable for a prolonged period. If it's a sibling who dies, both parents may become emotionally unavailable at a time when the child needs emotional support more than ever. As a result, essential lessons on emotion regulation may be lost, potentially delaying the development of this important skill.

Conclusion

Children's comprehension of death progresses in parallel with their overall development. When faced with death, they may display a level of understanding that surpasses their age. They advance from a rudimentary grasp of death's finality and irreversibility to a comprehensive understanding of its finite nature and the long-term effects of losing a loved one. The extent of their understanding is influenced by the level of care that they have received. Are they exposed to dialogue and openness, or is the opposite true? Do they live in an inclusive environment where they can partake in the events surrounding the death, or are they left on the sidelines, with just occasional glimpses into the adult world? Many factors, both personal and external, contribute to their development. In the patchwork of life experiences, it's important to have adults as companions and mentors. These adults, whether parents, educators, school personnel, therapists, or others, can lead children through this difficult transition in their lives.

Chapter 4

The Impact of Loss
on Children's Lives

Introduction

For centuries, researchers have been studying the effects of grief on adults, but it's only in recent years that the focus has shifted to understanding how children experience loss. While early studies relied on observations and assessments to gauge children's grief, contemporary research increasingly values children's perspectives and insights on their own experiences of bereavement.

This chapter provides a review of what we know about the consequences of childhood loss, with a particular emphasis on the effects of losing a parent or sibling. Although we have more research on parental loss than sibling loss, our examination encompasses the psychological, social, physical, and educational outcomes of bereavement in childhood. Our aim is to equip you with a better understanding of how grief can impact children's lives and the factors that can mitigate or increase the risks associated with childhood loss.

Psychological and social consequences

Most of us have encountered people who have experienced loss in their lives, and therefore we are familiar with the grief and difficult emotions that can accompany bereavement. It is natural to associate grief with a time of additional psychological stress. These apparent stressors have prompted researchers to investigate the nature and severity of the psychological reactions and difficulties that can arise as a result of bereavement. We now know that the loss of a close family member in childhood can cause significant problems for children, which can have lifelong consequences, particularly because children are so reliant on the adults around them. Death can interfere with and disrupt their cognitive and emotional development.

In this section, we look at the psychological and social consequences that can follow when a child loses a parent or sibling. We look at the psychological reactions that can occur immediately after the loss and the extent to which they continue in the years following and into adulthood. We also look at risk-taking behaviour, social challenges, life satisfaction, and suicide risk.

Psychological consequences after the loss

Researchers have found a consistent link between the loss of a parent or sibling and the risk of psychological consequences in the aftermath. Some of the most well-documented psychological reactions following a loss include fear, anger, insomnia, intrusive thoughts and memories, apathy, and psychosomatic symptoms[1] (Lytje & Dyregrov, 2019). For younger children in particular, the struggle of coping with a loss can further delay their development. John Coleman, an eminent paediatrician and professor at Oxford University, explains this delay by saying that when a child has to deal with something difficult (such as a death), there are other life challenges that must wait until the child has the energy to deal with them again (Coleman, 1978).

---

1   Psychosomatic disorders refer to physical symptoms, such as heart or breathing problems, or involuntary urination, that cannot be fully explained through medical examinations and are believed to be caused by psychological factors.

Several studies (Gray *et al.*, 2011; Worden, 1996) have found that guilt is often an overlooked but present challenge that grieving children may struggle with. In cases where siblings have been ill for long periods of time, it is not uncommon for the child, in a moment of frustration, to wish their ill sister or brother dead. Guilt may also arise if a parent is killed in an accident on the way to school or an after-school activity. Here, children's imaginations may turn to whether it was their fault. Children's feelings of guilt can also come out of the blue, for example when they think something has happened because they didn't tidy their room or spoke badly to their mum or dad. Such feelings of guilt seem to depend on how well the family shares the grief and talks about what has happened in the aftermath of the death (Worden, 1996). The better the family is at sharing grief with each other, the less likely it is that guilt will arise in the child, and the more likely it is that adults will take on the responsibility that children mistakenly assume.

Many researchers (e.g., Brent *et al.*, 2009; Dowdney, 2000) have been interested in investigating whether grief can be associated with an increased risk of developing depression. Several studies have now confirmed this association, but there is considerable disagreement about how high the risk is.

Pham and colleagues (2018) reported an increased risk for depression, particularly in the early stages of bereavement. Lin and colleagues (2004) found that up to 40% of bereaved children exhibited symptoms of clinical depression during the period following a loss. Other studies (Gersten *et al.*, 1991; Gray *et al.*, 2011) have found that the risk of depression is between 10% and 25%. However, some studies failed to discover any correlation between the loss of a family member and depression.

A large cohort study conducted by Høeg and colleagues (2023) in Denmark, which included all children born between 1987 and 2016 who had experienced the loss of a parent, found a concerning rise in the use of medication for psychological symptoms. The researchers observed a 59% higher risk of psychotropic medication prescription among bereaved male children compared to non-bereaved males, and a 56% higher risk among bereaved female children compared to non-bereaved females. The risk of receiving psychotropic medication was highest during the first six months after the loss and when the parent died within one year of diagnosis.

The findings in the existing literature on children's risk of depression following a loss display significant variation. There are several reasons that may account for such variation. First, the studies were conducted at different times and focused on different types of losses. It is plausible that the severity of a death, such as murder or witnessing a traumatic accident involving a family member, may increase the risk of developing psychological distress. Additionally, only in the last decade has there been a concerted effort to differentiate between children with complicated grief reactions and those with less complicated grief histories (see Chapter 6, Complicated Grief Processes). Finally, it is challenging to separate grief-specific effects from the potential impact of other life events on children's mental health. For instance, is it grief itself that leads to depression, or is it other consequences such as changing schools or interacting with peers who lack understanding of the situation? These factors highlight the complexity and multifaceted nature of the relationship between loss and children's mental health.

In addition to depression, a small number of studies have found evidence that children who lose a parent may be at increased risk of developing post-traumatic stress disorder (PTSD). Figures vary, but studies have found that up to 8.5% of children who lose a parent are at risk of this diagnosis (McClatchy *et al.*, 2009; Melhem *et al.*, 2008). Keulen and co-workers (2022) identified three subgroups in a study of 264 bereaved youths (aged 7–18): those with no post-traumatic stress (PTS) disturbance (37.9%), those with intermediate PTS disturbance (39.0%), and those with pervasive disturbance (23.1%). This means that more than 60% may struggle with problems due to traumatic after-effects. The authors comment that avoidance symptoms were most pronounced. From our clinical experience, we would add that children who experience violent losses such as murder or suicide are particularly at risk in this context, and only a minority (20.5%) of the bereaved youths had experienced such a loss. Avoidance may be expected when the emotional pain is high, but we agree with Keulen and co-workers that overuse of avoidance may interfere with cognitive and emotional processing of the loss.

Mental health consequences in adulthood

In the quest to understand the consequences of the loss of a family member, researchers have found that the negative consequences are not isolated to the time and years immediately following a death. Even in adulthood, people who have lost a close family member in childhood are at increased risk of developing mental disorders, including anxiety, bipolar disorder, clinical depression, and schizophrenia (Agid et al., 1999; e.g., Appel et al., 2016; Li et al., 2022; Mack, 2001).

A large Danish registry study was published in 2016 by Appel and colleagues. It examined whether increased use of antidepressant medications was seen in children and adults who had lost a parent. The study included more than 1 million Danes born between 1970 and 1990, of whom 71,380 had lost a parent when they were aged between 6 and 19 years old. The researchers found a significant increase in antidepressant use among adults who had lost a parent as a child. The younger they were when they experienced the loss, the greater their use of medication. Girls who had lost a parent to suicide were particularly hard hit. Appel and colleagues also found that medication use had not decreased two years after the death.

Otowa and colleagues (2014) further found a link between parental loss and the risk of developing later alcohol abuse and phobias.[2] As with many other areas of children's grief, there is still

---

2   Phobias are anxiety disorders characterized by intense, disproportionate fear triggered by specific situations or objects. They may interfere with daily activities and result in avoidance behaviour.

a lack of knowledge and understanding of exactly how parental loss plays into mental health disorders. However, the reported studies fit very well with the findings of more general studies on stressful life events and the risk of developing mental disorders.

Self-harm and suicide risk

For some children, the experience of loss can be so distressing that it can lead to self-harm and suicide attempts. Jørgensen and colleagues (2019) found that there was a 7% increased risk of self-harming behaviour among students who had experienced loss in grades 7–10 (approximate ages 13–16) and a 10% increased risk among students in upper secondary school (approximate ages 16–20). Regarding suicidal ideation, young people in grades 7–10 who had experienced loss had a 9% higher risk of suicidal ideation, while the figure among upper secondary students was 10%. However, only the results from upper secondary students were significant. In practice, this means that although the study found a difference, it may not reflect other age groups.

These results have been supported by other studies. Research conducted by Nielsen and colleagues (2012) found that among 3481 individuals aged 15–24, of which 1212 had lost a parent or sibling, 23.1% of the bereaved participants had considered suicide, compared to 14.5% of children from intact homes. Furthermore, 7.3 of participants from bereaved families had attempted suicide, compared to 3.3% of participants from intact homes. The risk of suicide was thus twice as high among participants who had experienced loss. International studies have confirmed this trend and found that the risk increases if the cause of death is unnatural – that is, not due to illness or age. Unnatural causes of death may include traffic accidents, suicide, and murder.

International researchers have managed to remove social stressors (such as low income, poor health, and risky behaviour) from their studies, and even after they are removed, an increased risk is still observed. Niederkrotenthaler and colleagues (2012) found that the risk of suicide attempts is higher the younger the child is when the death occurs. This has led them to recommend early intervention in homes where children experience loss at a young age. Sandler and co-workers (2021) found grief as a predictor for long-term risk for suicidal ideation and attempts in parentally bereaved children and adolescents.

High-risk behaviour

When children and young people engage in risky behaviour, such as taking drugs, committing crimes, or drinking too much alcohol, it puts them at risk for poor physical and psychological health. Several studies have found a clear link between such behaviours and the loss of a parent or sibling.

The previously mentioned study by Nielsen and colleagues (2012) found that 36% of bereaved children smoked regularly compared to 21% of non-bereaved children. At the same time, 53% of bereaved children had experience with euphoriant drugs compared to 34% of non-bereaved children. The study by Jørgensen and colleagues (2019) found similar results. Here, it was reported that among bereaved children, 6% in grades 7–10 smoked, while 7% smoked in secondary school. The difference in young people who had smoked cannabis was a modest 2% higher in grades 7–10, while the difference was 10% higher among bereaved than among non-bereaved young people in secondary education. This is consistent with a general societal trend: the older the children are, the riskier their behaviour. These findings mirror international research, which has also found that sudden and severe losses often lead to increased risk-taking behaviour among bereaved children (Cross, 2002; Worden, 1996).

Nielsen and colleagues (2012) further found a link between crime and the loss of a family member. They reported that 34.7% of bereaved children had committed crimes such as assault and burglary. This was 7% higher than in the control group. At the same time, the study found a very small, yet worrying, increased tendency for girls from bereaved families to be subjected to incest or sexual abuse by close family members. This was reported by 5.9% of the female participants experiencing loss compared to 1.1% of the control group. Although this was a very small group overall, it is worth noting that the risk of being subjected to incest was five times higher for girls from homes with deaths in the immediate family. In their study, Jørgensen and colleagues (2019) found no difference in the level of crime committed by bereaved pupils in grades 7–10. However, they did find a 33% increased tendency for bereaved young people to subsequently commit crimes while in secondary education.

Social consequences

While researchers have been most interested in the psychological consequences of loss, studies on the social consequences have been less widespread. However, there is now a consensus that the challenges that arise in the aftermath of a loss can be as significant as the loss itself. This includes issues such as changes in family income, depression in the remaining parent, and reduced parenting capacity. Here it is particularly important that the children left behind have responsible adults and supportive friends around them so that negative consequences can be minimized. Especially in the case of older children, the support of friends is important.

From the above perspective, it is problematic that the study by Nielsen and colleagues (2012) found that one in five bereaved children had not spoken to anyone about their loss. However, Jørgensen and co-workers (2019) found a more positive picture in their study. Here, there was no difference between bereaved children and their classmates in terms of whether they felt they could confide in friends. However, only 63% of bereaved pupils felt that their classmates accepted them as they were, compared to 74% of children from intact homes. Fortunately, this levelled out when pupils entered secondary education.

In Norway, K. Dyregrov and A. Dyregrov (2011) studied children's relationships with their peers after the loss of a parent to cancer. They found that the bereaved children were often left with a feeling of having lost their sense of belonging to their peer group. This was consistent with an earlier study by the same researchers, in which they interviewed children who had lost siblings to suicide. Here, participants in the study often described their friends as childish, immature, and focused on irrelevant and meaningless things (K. Dyregrov & A. Dyregrov, 2005). At the same time, several participants reported a feeling of unease in their bodies when interacting with other people. Their experience of loss made them uncertain about developing close relationships with others because they were afraid that they might end up dying from loved ones. Evidence suggests that this fear is particularly present in children who experience suicide.

Høeg and colleagues (2018) found that the loss of a parent was generally associated with a higher chance of finding a partner later in life for young women, but not for young men. However, the incidence of divorce was also higher among both men and women who had lost a parent or sibling as children. Further, divorce was more likely among those who had lost a parent to suicide.

Life satisfaction and future outlook

Researchers have long questioned whether loss in childhood can lead to reduced happiness in adulthood. This is difficult to investigate as it is difficult to isolate the consequences of loss from other life factors (e.g., upbringing, socio-economic factors) that also affect how children develop.

Few studies have addressed this, but the previously reported study by Jørgensen and colleagues (2019) found that there was no significantly greater concern about their own health among children in grades 7–10 who had experienced the loss of a close family member. In secondary education, however, the picture was different. Here, 40% of bereaved young people had concerns about their own health, compared with 28% of young people from intact families.

Concerns about having children themselves were also 6% higher among bereaved young people in secondary education. Here, 26% had concerns about having children, while the figure was only 20% among children who still had both parents.

In an English study, Parsons (2011) found that concerns about the future persisted well into adulthood, based on a survey of 534 adults who had lost a parent before the age of 16. The study found that those left behind were likely to express that they 'did not get out of life what they wanted' (2011, p.11). At the same time, they had an increased risk of being unemployed by the age of 30.

Physical and health consequences

Many professionals and laypeople who have interacted with those who are grieving can attest to the significant mental impact that grief can have. While much research has focused on the psychological consequences of bereavement, there are instances where children experiencing grief may also exhibit physical symptoms such as headaches, eating problems, or stomach aches, as noted in various studies (Liu *et al.*, 2013; Nielsen *et al.*, 2012; Van Eerdewegh *et al.*, 1985). This raises the question of whether grief can also have physical health implications. Although few studies have examined this, this section delves into what has been discovered in greater depth.

Physical reactions

Some studies have revealed that certain children may be vulnerable to a range of physical health issues following a loss, such as headaches, asthma, loss of appetite, difficulty concentrating, and muscle pain. These physical challenges may progress from temporary to chronic. Bylund-Grenklo and colleagues (2016) conducted a study in Sweden, examining the aftermath of losing a parent at 13–16 years of age. Six to nine years after the loss, 49% of the participants reported unresolved grief, with physical symptoms such as insomnia and persistent exhaustion. However, several studies have not found similar health effects, and the lack of consensus and research on the topic makes it challenging to determine to what extent physical consequences play a role in the aftermath of a loss. Nevertheless, in practical settings, it is not uncommon to come across children and young people who struggle with complaints like headaches or insomnia after a bereavement.

Health consequences

It has been found that children who have lost a close family member in childhood generally have more health issues than children from intact families. Two US researchers (Luecken, 2008; Luecken & Roubinov, 2012) further found that while health issues are short term for the vast majority, 10–21% experience persistent health problems. That health problems can become long term has been confirmed in other studies (Burrell *et al.*, 2022; Pham *et al.*, 2018), which have further found that children who experience unexpected deaths (e.g., suicide or car accident) are at even greater risk for long-term health issues.

A study by Parsons (2011) revealed that females who experienced the loss of a parent during childhood reported having fair or average health, but not excellent health. Additionally, 4% of men from bereaved families reported being permanently sick or disabled and not working at the age of 30. Although this percentage is not substantial, it is double the 2% of men from intact families who reported the same.

From a Scandinavian perspective, the Danish study by Jørgensen and colleagues (2019) found that fewer bereaved children generally reported being in good health compared to their classmates. In primary school this was 11% and in secondary education 5%.

From a medical standpoint, studies have demonstrated that the body experiences significant stress during major life events, such as the loss of a parent or sibling (Dietz *et al.*, 2013). The body's production of stress hormones increases, which can lead to long-term physical and psychological changes. Overproduction of stress hormones has, in some studies (e.g. Kivimäki & Steptoe, 2018; Vaccarino et al., 2021; Virk et al., 2016), been associated with the development of several physical diseases, such as diabetes and heart diseases. It has also been associated with the development of psychopathological challenges, such as depression and anxiety (Merz & Wolf, 2022; van Praag, 2004).

In a study examining the impact of parental loss during childhood on conscripted men in Sweden, Kennedy and colleagues (2018) found that men who experienced such a loss had a 49% higher risk of having low stress-coping thresholds compared to conscripts from intact families. If the loss was a father, the risk increased to 79%. However, the study could not determine whether the increased risk was due to the loss itself or to events that occurred in the aftermath.

Mortality and suicide risk

In the last decade, several researchers have been interested in whether childhood losses have any impact on how long you live. In scientific circles, this is referred to as the general mortality of grief and is understood here as the risk that a person who has experienced a loss in childhood will die prematurely, regardless of the cause of death. General mortality can thus be caused by dying from a disease (e.g., cancer), in an accident, or by suicide.

Li and colleagues (2014) conducted a large-scale study to investigate whether the overall mortality rate increases for individuals who experience the loss of a parent during childhood. Their extensive study encompassed individuals born in Denmark, Sweden, and Finland. The authors discovered that those who had lost a parent during childhood had a 50% higher risk of premature death in adulthood than individuals from intact families. This risk increased even further if the parent had died unnaturally, such as through suicide, car accidents, or murder. Other studies, including by Rostila and Saarela (2011) and Smith and colleagues (2014), have reported similar findings.

It's worth noting that while the risk increase is significant, the study does not provide insight into how much shorter the life expectancy is for those who have experienced parental loss during childhood. It remains unclear whether these individuals die years, months, weeks, or days earlier than those who have not lost a parent in childhood. From discussions with researchers in the field, it seems that the difference is more likely a matter of months than years. Li and colleagues (2014) also found that those who were very young at the time of the parental loss were particularly vulnerable to premature death. The authors speculate that this may be linked to reduced care in the immediate aftermath of the death. For babies and young children, a lack of care during this period can be particularly dangerous, as they are unable to feed themselves or communicate pain or illness, except through crying.

Rostila and colleagues (Hiyoshi *et al.*, 2017; 2021) have demonstrated that the increased mortality risk associated with childhood loss also applies to individuals who have lost siblings. Their Swedish register study found that this trend was more pronounced if the sibling who died was not a baby (younger than one year) or if the death occurred during adolescence (between 12 and 18 years).

It is not only the risk of dying prematurely that increases after the loss of a parent. Unfortunately, there also seems to be a link between childhood loss and an increased risk of suicide. In this perspective, Guldin and colleagues (2015) investigated a possible association between having lost a parent and an increased risk of suicidality among children born in Denmark, Sweden, and Finland. They found that the risk of dying from suicide was twice as high for children who had lost a parent, regardless of the cause of death. For children who had lost a parent to suicide, the risk was three times higher. This group of children had an 82% higher risk of taking their own life than children who had lost a parent in an accident. Unfortunately, the tendency for children who lose a parent to suicide to die from suicide themselves has been confirmed in other studies (Niederkrotenthaler *et al.*, 2012; Rostila *et al.*, 2016). Similarly, there are indications that younger children are particularly at risk here (Niederkrotenthaler *et al.*, 2012).

The research clearly shows that the stress of losing a parent or sibling in childhood can cast a shadow over adult life. But here too we must mention that statistics can be frightening, and the shortened life expectancy is probably a few months out of such a lifetime. The large number of people involved in the study makes it easier to obtain statistically significant results.

Educational consequences

Children spend a significant amount of their time in educational institutions, making schools very important in their lives. However, when a child is dealing with grief, it can significantly affect their ability to concentrate and perform in school. Although some children find comfort in the structure and routine of school, the emotional weight of loss can permeate their academic performance and overall well-being.

What exactly happens to a child's education when they lose a loved one? Can they continue to keep up with their studies? And do they have the same opportunities for success as their non-bereaved peers in the future? We will now explore these questions, delving into the impact of loss on education and the potential long-term consequences for bereaved children.

Concentration and performance at school

One of the consequences most people will associate with loss is the grief and the difficult and many thoughts that go with it. This can affect concentration and performance. Over the last two decades, there has been a lot of research into the well-being of bereaved children at school. However, the quality of this research has been variable, resulting in many inconsistent and contradictory findings.

A number of studies have reported that, compared to their classmates, bereaved children generally have an increased risk of underachievement at school (Berg *et al.*, 2014; Høeg *et al.*, 2019; Kailaheimo-Lönnqvist & Kotimäki, 2020). Other studies have concluded that achievement varies widely and that some bereaved pupils actually perform better in the post-loss period. However, recent studies have generally confirmed an increased risk of children performing worse at school after experiencing a loss. This is often attributed to concentration problems and the intrusion of difficult thoughts in the aftermath. Overachievement is attributed to the fact that schoolwork can act as a defence mechanism, giving the child a place to escape to and think about other things. Some researchers have also argued that overachievement can be seen as a way for the bereaved child to honour the deceased by making something of themselves and achieving good results.

Concentration problems are a frequently reported challenge, as studies with bereaved children and teachers' reports (A. Dyregrov *et al.*, 2015a; Lytje, 2016b; Nielsen *et al.*, 2012; Holland, 2003) have pointed out. The challenge is most often in subjects that require close attention. Here, it is not only thoughts and intrusive memories of the loss itself that can play a role in concentration – problems in the family, such as depression in the remaining parent or economic challenges, lead to additional worries and thoughts. Similarly, other factors such as regressive behaviour[3], increased absenteeism from school, and reduced self-esteem can affect performance. Although we now know that loss can lead to learning difficulties, we know much less about why this is the case.

Educational level and future prospects

Over the past two decades, many research studies have examined how losing a family member during childhood affects a child's future education and opportunities. One study conducted by Parsons in 2011 focused on children who had lost a mother or father before

---

3   Regressive behaviour can be defined as a return to a previous, less-developed stage of a psychological developmental phase.

they turned 16 years old. The study found that these children had more difficulties performing in school and had fewer aspirations for their future compared to peers who had not experienced such a loss.

This difficulty in school and lower motivation affected both boys and girls, but boys were found to be more vulnerable. As a result, troubled students who had experienced such a loss were more likely to drop out or be expelled from school.

Parsons also found, as described earlier, an increased risk of unemployment by the age of 30, and that people who had lost a parent or sibling as children were under-represented in leadership positions. International studies have confirmed these trends and further found that children who have experienced bereavement have lower aspirations for their own education and careers (Brent *et al.*, 2012; Worden, 1996). However, research also suggests that if the pupil has previously had high academic achievement and positive self-esteem, this may compensate for some of the risks mentioned (Prix & Erola, 2017).

A large Danish study by Høeg and colleagues (2019), which included the entire Danish population born in the period 1982–2000, further examined the educational consequences for children who lost a parent before the age of 18. The study found that the probability of these children achieving a certain level of education was as much as 5% lower for primary and secondary school and 26% lower for university studies compared to statistics for children who had not lost a parent. Boys were also more likely than girls not to realize their educational potential.

Høeg and co-workers' investigation did not furnish substantial insights regarding the underlying reasons for the challenges observed. The findings from Jørgensen and colleagues' research (2019), however, may offer explanations. According to the study, disengaged pupils in secondary education showed an 11% greater tendency to miss school due to illness in the previous month. In addition, 55% of pupils in grades 7–10 who had experienced bereavement needed to consult a psychologist, compared to 29%

of their peers. This need was even more pronounced in secondary education, where 62% of bereaved pupils had sought psychological help, in contrast to 30% of their classmates. Difficulties with concentration, increased absenteeism, and psychological distress requiring treatment may be indicative of the persisting impact of childhood losses.

Burrell and colleagues (2020) used records from Norway and looked at children who lost their parents suddenly from external causes (suicide, accidents, murder) before the age of 18. They found that these children were disadvantaged in terms of completing any education, including university or other higher education. The study found no differences in the causes of death, gender, or the time of death of the parent in childhood.

However, there are also studies that have found no association between the loss of a parent and educational attainment. One of these was by Prix and Erola (2017). It was based on children who had lost a father and concluded that these children did not drop out of secondary education as long as the remaining mother had strong socio-economic resources. However, the young people left behind performed worse at university compared to their peers who had not experienced parental loss.

Berg and colleagues (2014) conducted a study that demonstrated a strong correlation between socio-economic status and academic struggles among children and adolescents. Specifically, pupils who had experienced the loss of a parent exhibited lower academic performance. However, the authors found that the fluctuations in academic performance were primarily attributed to pre-existing social and familial characteristics in the child's life, rather than the loss itself. In other words, challenges stemming from the child's difficult family background were more predictive of subsequent difficulties after the loss than the loss itself. Other research (Ribbens McCarthy with Jessop, 2005) has also indicated that children from low socio-economic households are more susceptible to experiencing parental loss, which is often linked to social inequalities in health, such as lower education and poor health. Therefore, children from disadvantaged socio-economic backgrounds not only face an increased risk of experiencing heightened grief symptoms, but also are more likely to lose a parent. These findings suggest that while bereaved young people are more susceptible to lower educational attainment, many of the difficulties they face may additionally stem from pre-existing issues within the family, which may be increased by the loss, even if they are not directly caused by it.

Gender differences in coping with childhood bereavement

While the gender differences between boys and girls during the early years of a child's life may not be significant, in our practice we experience more parents reporting that even before starting school, boys may be less inclined to discuss a death they have experienced, less likely to express their emotions, and more prone to avoid conversations than girls. However, it is important to stress that individual differences may be greater than gender differences.

Gender differences become more evident as the child reaches school age and beyond, and are particularly pronounced in adolescence. In an article we have written on children's reactions after the murder of their teacher, we describe how girls experienced various grief and crisis reactions afterwards, to a much greater extent than boys (A. Dyregrov, 1988). The girls cried much more, experienced concentration difficulties more often, and were more frightened and anxious than the boys. Only in one area did the boys report a stronger reaction than the girls: they tried harder to push away thoughts of what had happened. We also found differences in how the boys and girls conveyed their feelings in written form. For example, in response to open-ended questions in a short questionnaire, the girls described in relative detail how they first reacted, what made the biggest impression on them, and so on, while the boys gave short answers and did little to put their feelings into words.

Other studies (Bylund-Grenklo *et al.*, 2021; Stikkelbroek *et al.*, 2016) have also concluded that girls appear to be more at risk of struggling over time and internalizing their grief than boys.

The girls in our aforementioned study (A. Dyregrov, 1988) also reported talking about the death at home to a greater extent than boys. Although these are not children who have lost a close friend, sibling, or parent, we have seen a familiar pattern emerge over time: that boys are less likely than girls to recognize or experience grief and crisis reactions, and that they are much less likely to process such experiences through conversations.

Gender differences are also reflected in studies of grief, where, for example, girls in adolescence tend to struggle more with so-called internalizing problems such as anxiety, sadness and depression, post-traumatic symptoms, and so on, than boys. However, the two genders differ to a lesser extent in terms of problem behaviours or externalizing problems (Shulla & Toomey, 2018). In one of the few studies that followed children for a long time (20 years) after parental loss, the chances of developing major depression in adulthood were elevated only among females (Reinherz *et al.*, 1999). Given that girls talk to others more and find it easier to put their feelings into words, one would think that they would be better equipped to cope with loss and trauma, but it is usually not that simple. Where gender differences exist, it is almost always girls who react most strongly and for the longest time.

The reasons for these differences in reactions are probably to be found in several areas. It is well known that boys and girls have a different experience of play and friendships. Girls play more in pairs and are preoccupied with expressive play, which in itself absorbs the close human and interpersonal aspects of life. Through play they learn a language of emotions. Boys' play consists more in learning to fit in with the group, to abide by rules, and not to show emotion. Outside play, social learning and education are also different for different genders, so boys and girls can acquire different 'skills' in relation to their emotions.

Cautiously and somewhat speculatively, it is also possible that different genders have developed different abilities to deal with death and danger through evolution. Boys and men seem to have an easier time pushing things away, looking ahead, and not dwelling on emotions, while girls and women are more adept at confronting emotions. Grief professionals believe that the explanation for girls' stronger reactions lies in the fact that they are more sensitive to stress in the family, are more concerned about other family members (e.g., bereaved parents), and feel greater responsibility in the family. The approach to emotions that they develop in childhood also makes them closer to their feelings. These are some of the different and probably interacting explanations for gender differences. For a more detailed discussion, see Rose and Rudolph (2006).

Whatever the reason, it is important to be aware of these gender differences among children when helping them. Unfortunately, our ways of helping children in grief seem to be better adapted to girls' responses than boys'. Help is based on relatively direct conversations about emotional reactions, which seem easier for girls than for boys. For many boys, it is less natural to put their experiences into words and they may express different aspects of their experience through concrete activities. For boys, alternative methods can be used. The use of practical working tools that make it easier for children to communicate their experiences, impressions, thoughts, and reactions can also help us to reach boys. Such methods range from systematic writing tasks, to pictures that are easy to create stories about, to drawings in which children can colour in the emotional state they are experiencing or indicate when in the day they experience the most difficult thoughts or feelings (Straume, 1999).

Conclusion

In conclusion, this chapter has aimed to provide a comprehensive overview of the diverse and far-reaching consequences that may arise from the loss of a parent or sibling. While extensive research has shed light on some of the potential effects of grief, our understanding of this complex and multifaceted phenomenon remains incomplete. Notably, the implications of children's grief and its outcomes are still poorly understood and require further investigation. Regrettably, researchers have often relied on the assumption that children's grief is analogous to that of adults, despite the unique developmental, experiential, and social factors that shape the experiences of grieving children. This tendency is concerning, as it may overlook the distinctive needs of young individuals and impede the provision of appropriate and effective support.

Hence, this chapter highlights the high importance of recognizing and addressing the diverse impacts of grief across various domains of children's lives. Indeed, the effects of children's grief can reverberate across a range of areas, including mental health, social relationships, and even mortality. Therefore, it is essential to prioritize further research to deepen our understanding of the nature of children's grief and its consequences. By doing so, we can enhance our capacity to provide targeted and effective interventions that mitigate the harmful effects of grief and promote children's well-being.

Chapter 5

Types of Loss

Introduction: Different losses lead to different challenges

Grief, sadness, and mourning will always be integral parts of being bereaved as a child. However, the thoughts, worries, and reactions that come with different types of loss can vary widely. Research shows that grief experiences can differ according to the type of loss (Brent *et al.*, 2012; K. Dyregrov & A. Dyregrov, 2005), so it is not unusual for children who lose a parent to face different challenges from those who lose a close friend.

The aim of this chapter is to provide you with the knowledge to recognize and address the unique situations that arise when children experience the loss of a parent, sibling, or friend. We will explore the range of support measures that may be required following sudden death or life-threatening illness. By delving into the intricacies of various types of loss, we hope to provide a nuanced understanding of how different crises demand different forms of support. Our goal is to help you appreciate the subtleties of grief and enhance your ability to provide tailored and effective support to children in their time of need.

Loss of a parent

When a parent dies, a child loses one of the most important people in their life. Parents are not just central to providing physical care and a roof over their heads. They are also guides, mentors, and life companions. For many of us, it is our parents who teach us to ride a bike, tie our shoelaces, and help us find our place in the world. So when a child loses a parent, the loss is twofold: in that moment, the child loses one of the most important carers in their life – and in the long term, they lose all the future guidance and care that person would have provided. It therefore makes sense that research (Alahakoon, 2018; Li *et al.*, 2014) has found particularly strong consequences of parental loss, both in the period immediately after the loss, but also well into adulthood. We described this earlier in Chapter 4 (The Impact of Loss on Children's Lives).

Often, the specific challenges that may arise following the loss of a parent depend on the age of the child at the time of death. For very young children, there may be a risk that general care will deteriorate. Studies (Li *et al.*, 2014; Rostila & Saarela, 2011) have shown that this is particularly a risk in unexpected and violent losses (e.g., suicide or a car accident), where the remaining parent is in shock and deep grief. These emotions can very naturally lead to the remaining parent not being able to provide the same care to the child as before the death, for a period of time.

There may be times during the grieving process when the remaining parent feels overwhelmed and unable to attend to all of the needs of the bereaved child. As one parent we interviewed put it:

'Suddenly you feel more alone than you ever did. Because the person you've built your whole world around is suddenly gone. You have to be a good father, you have to make ends meet, you have to do all these things. All of a sudden you're on your own and there's no one to talk to.' *A dad*

If the remaining parent does not have a strong support network, the worst-case scenario could be a dangerous situation for very young children in particular, who may not receive necessary medical attention if the parent is overwhelmed by grief. Research has found that children who lose a parent at a young age are at a higher risk of distress and premature death than those for whom it happens at an older age (Li *et al.*, 2014; Rostila & Saarela, 2011; Smith *et al.*, 2014).

While older children can be less dependent on general care, they may face their own unique difficulties. In some cases, and especially in large families with many siblings, there may be a need to take on tasks from the deceased adult. These might include activities such as cleaning, cooking, shopping, and looking after younger siblings. Although there is nothing wrong with the family helping each other, it can become a problem if the children become 'little adults', sometimes termed 'parentified children'.

If the new burdens mean they have no time for homework, interests, or seeing friends, there is cause for concern. Some children also start to change their behaviour and spend more time at home, because they may be afraid that the remaining parent will become lonely. It is important that you, as a professional, ask about and form a picture of the role of the child in the home, as the 'little adults' are often much harder to detect than children who continue their usual social life. At the same time, these children will often be happy to help out at home and may refer to it as being okay. However, this does not mean that they do not also miss being with friends and participating in extracurricular activities. Here, adult support may be needed to help the child find a balance between helping out at home and being allowed to be a child.

As a professional working with children, your main responsibility is to prioritize the well-being of the bereaved child. However, as a friend or acquaintance, you may be more focused on compensating for the child's problems or shortcomings. In either role, it's important to understand the situation of the remaining parent, as their situation directly impacts the child's well-being.

The loss of a loved one is difficult for everyone, including the remaining parent or partner, who has also lost a key person in their life. Both emotionally and practically, they are affected by the void left behind. While there is often support available for children's well-being, there is much less focus on support for the remaining parent in this scenario. Many parents are unsure of what support their children need and may have concerns about whether their children's grief reactions are 'right' or 'wrong', and how to deal with grief as a family. Regardless of their resources, every parent wants the best for their children. If you have the energy to listen and offer advice, or if you know of a place that offers counselling for adults in grief, it can be very helpful to pass this on to the parent. Support organizations for those who have lost a spouse or partner may be of special importance as they provide experience from those who have lived through a similar loss.

It is important to note that many children today do not live in a 'traditional' family with a mother and father. Blended families, divorced parents, and same-sex parents are increasingly common. In the case of a blended family, for example, the loss of a parent may not necessarily result in a shared bereavement within the family. If the child's parents divorced many years ago and the divorce was unhappy, it is not certain that the mother will grieve the death of the father. This situation can make it difficult for the child to find a space to grieve and remember the deceased parent, and they may have no one to share their grief with. It is important that other adults step in and create a safe space for the child to open up about their grief. Here are some helpful tips for dealing with parental death:

- Despite the child's difficult situation, consider whether there are areas where you are particularly concerned for the bereaved child. This could be in relation to friendships or academic underachievement. Accept that although you cannot magically remove the child's grief, you can help the child with specific challenges.

- Give the child the opportunity to have some private conversations (just the two of you), where there is time and space to talk about what is difficult. Consider what setting is best for the specific child, such as during a craft activity or on a walk.

- If you are unsure how the child's remaining parent is handling the situation, try to ask about it through open-ended questions. For example: 'How does Mum feel about Dad's death?' or 'Do you talk about Dad at home?'

Sibling loss

Loss of siblings has been called 'the forgotten grief'. Most people can relate to the huge life change of losing a parent, but the same is not always true of losing a sibling. For outsiders, sibling loss can be difficult to relate to and is often seen as less problematic than parental loss. However, the extent to which siblings influence and shape each other, for better or worse, should not be underestimated. At the same time, the relationship with a sister or brother is often far more complex than that we have with a parent. Often, sibling relationships are made up of strongly ambivalent feelings. On the one hand, the child loves their sister or brother, while on the other hand, there are often elements of frustration and rivalry. Because siblings are so secure in their relationship, they rarely have problems showing and expressing both positive and negative emotions to each other. Arguments as well as good experiences are therefore natural and expressed parts of most sibling relationships. This ambivalence makes the relationship between two siblings unique compared to other relationships in our lives.

The complexity of sibling relationships means that the loss of a sibling can often lead to significant feelings of guilt in the remaining child (Brooten *et al.*, 2018; Funk *et al.*, 2018). If, in the period leading up to the death, siblings have quarrelled a lot and have not resolved the conflict, this can further complicate the grief of the child. In cases of serious illness, there will often be a long period before the death in which the ill sibling receives most of the parents' attention – and this can lead to frustration for the healthy child at the lack of care and attention given to them.

Siblings may even think that everything would be easier if the ailing sister or brother died. Such thoughts can cause a great deal of guilt after the death. Younger children in particular, but also older ones, may think that their wish was the direct cause of the death (known as 'magical thinking') – that the death occurred because they wanted it to happen. Frustration at the lack of attention and care may also lead to the child feeling relief at the death, in addition to grief. This feeling is quite natural, but may haunt the remaining child in the aftermath.

The need for the remaining child to take over practical tasks is less the case with sibling loss than with parental loss, as both parents are still available. However, the child may still feel that the parents' grief is so heavy that there is a need for them to help with practical tasks. At the same time, some parents may be so preoccupied with their own grief that they do not have the time to support the remaining child. One child we spoke to recounted such an experience. She found that her parents believed the grief of losing their child as greater than her loss of a sibling. They thus made their grieving process private and excluded her from participating in it. She still resented this many years later. In other cases, such exclusion may occur because the parents want to protect the child and not make him or her sadder. However, both situations are problematic as the child is not getting the support they need.

At the same time, it is also important to remember that a person who had an important role in the family is now gone. For example, if the deceased sister or brother was better at school, remaining siblings may feel that they now have to fill some shoes that they are not capable of stepping into. In some cases, there is also an idolization of the deceased, with all the positive qualities highlighted and the negative aspects forgotten. One boy told us that the worst thing he had experienced was the idolization of his brother. He had known his brother when he was very young and could not remember much about their time together. At the same time, he knew that the glorified stories told by his parents were only part of the truth. Without also knowing his brother's negative and annoying sides, the boy felt he never really came to understand who he had been. The boy was left with only a glossy image. The idolization can also lead to situations where the remaining child feels that they must live up to impossible standards in order to be as loved as the deceased.

As can be seen in the examples above, sibling relationships both before and after death are often very complex. It is therefore important that you understand the difficult thoughts that may arise in the aftermath of the loss, and which may feel shameful to talk about. Few children will tell you, without prompting, how they felt relieved by the death of their ill sibling. Many children who lose a sister or brother are not even asked about the loss, which is problematic. Our basic position should be that children who lose a sibling have just as much right to support and can have just as difficult grief reactions as children who lose a parent. Here we have listed some specific advice on sibling loss:

- Remember that the loss of a sibling can be just as impactful as the loss of a parent, and that the surviving child also needs extra attention and support in the aftermath.

- Assess how the family communicates and copes with the loss at home. This will help you understand whether the child is included in the grieving process or feels isolated in their grief. If you notice any difficulties, consider reaching out to the family (with the child's consent) and offering assistance in establishing a support framework for coping and discussing grief.

- Talk with the affected child. Let them know that it is not uncommon for children to think they are to blame for their sibling's death or to have negative thoughts or feelings about them. These comments can serve as a starting point for discussing the child's experiences and feelings.

Loss of friends

While the death of a sibling can be an unappreciated loss, the same can be true when children lose a friend. The loss of a friend is often seen as less complex and traumatic than when children lose a family member. The consequence is that there is frequently much less external support available for bereaved children in such situations. However, studies have shown that in some cases the loss of a friend can be as difficult as losing a parent or sibling. Researchers have found that the loss of a close friend can be a life-changing event that has major consequences for the child's development (Balk *et al.*, 2011; Doka, 2013).

It is therefore problematic that in bereavement groups we rarely observe children who have lost a friend. One explanation for this may be a lack of external attention to this type of loss because the bereaved child's family remains intact. This may create an expectation that any challenges are something that the home will take care of. However, this approach is problematic as some families do not have the resources to deal with the child's crisis or lack the necessary understanding of how such a loss can take a toll on their child.

The amount of support that children receive after the loss of a friend can depend on factors such as the location of the relationship and how well known it is at school. Research has shown that in Scandinavia, many schools hold memorial services and provide grief counselling after a loss (A. Dyregrov *et al.*, 1999a; Lytje, 2016a). In contrast, studies conducted in British schools (e.g., Holland, 1993, 2000; Lowton & Higginson, 2003) have found that grieving children often receive less support. This may be attributed to the fact that most British schools do not have a pre-planned approach for how to deal with bereavement.

Memorial services, when done right, allow both the class and the deceased pupil's friends to grieve together and create an important shared story about the loss. However, such support rarely reaches all of the child's friends. It can be particularly difficult for those who were not in the same class or even school as the deceased and who therefore risk being overlooked. This can lead to problematic situations, such as when the loss is passed on to other classes. One pupil talks about this:

> 'My teacher spoke to the whole class. He only said that he [the friend] had died and that he was sorry, to those who had known him. I had tears in my eyes, but I didn't cry. Then someone said, "Look at K.H.", and several of my classmates turned to me. The teacher asked if anyone knew him [the friend], but it was a bit difficult to say that I knew him. I just wanted to be alone. I should have stayed at home that day, but I was at school all day.'

Researchers have also suggested that gender may play a role and that the loss of a friend is often more difficult for girls than for boys (Coleman, 2011; De Goede *et al.*, 2009; Malone, 2012). This may be because girls define themselves more through friendships, while boys are more focused on asserting themselves and showing independence.

As with other types of loss, the loss of a friend can complicate the child's other friendships. However, the fact that the loss is rarely considered as serious as the loss of a family member creates a much higher risk that friends will not receive advice and support on how to deal with the bereaved friend. This can make some friends so insecure that they choose to withdraw from the friendship. For those friends who stay, the bereaved person's grief is often seen as a process that has a beginning and an end point. Friends may therefore be afraid to say or do anything that might interrupt or prolong the grieving process (Winther-Lindqvist & Olund Larsen, 2021). Such concerns make them very sensitive to the needs of the bereaved friend and may lead to their own concerns and needs being pushed to the background. This situation breeds unbalanced friendships that can be difficult to maintain in the long term. When friends die, it is therefore a good idea to pay particular attention to the following:

- The loss of a friend can complicate relationships with other friends who did not know the deceased. Check with the affected child whether they need help to talk about this with friends.

- Unfortunately, not everyone may understand the severity of losing a friend. It is important to ask the bereaved young person if they are facing any difficulties with specific groups, such as their family, class, or other friends. This can help identify areas where additional support may be needed.

Specific challenges related to circumstances of the loss

In this chapter, we have reviewed three of the most common types of loss that children are likely to experience in childhood. Although these losses are all powerful and life-changing events, they are far from being the only losses children face in childhood. Losses of grandparents, peripheral family members, family friends, and pets are far more common and affect almost everyone before adulthood. The majority of these losses are something that the child and their family go through. In addition, many children experience the divorce of their parents, which will also trigger loss reactions. Regardless, children's grief responses are as unique as their personalities, and losses are shaped by the everyday lives they live in.

You can therefore rarely base your expectations of a child's grief reaction on which person has died. For a child from a home with alcohol problems, where the family dog was always there when mum and dad fought, the death of the dog may be more upsetting than the loss of grandparents they rarely saw. The child's grief reactions are always based on the history and relationship they had with the deceased. This can make the loss easier than expected, but it can also make it harder. That's why it's important to always approach a child's own experience of loss with curiosity. By asking open-ended questions, you can find out if there are any particular concerns and what support the child needs.

The circumstances of a loss can also help to define when and how to intervene. In the case of a death preceded by a long period of life-threatening illness, children may also have special support needs in the run-up to the death. In the case of sudden death, there may be such strong traumatic elements that children may need specialized help. The final section of this chapter looks at these two specific challenges.

Life-threatening illness

In a previous study we conducted (Lytje, 2016b), bereaved Danish children shared their experiences of how the time before the death could be just as difficult as the time after the loss. Even though the death was painful and marked by intense grief, it also brought an end to a period full of fear and uncertainty. Before the death, everyday life was often consumed with worries about the health of the ill person and the possibility of a relapse. In cases of parental illness, there was a sudden lack of an adult for both social and practical activities. In cases of sibling illness, one adult was often with the ailing child in the hospital, leaving the remaining family members to cope on their own. Such burdens can put families in a difficult situation as they often create chaotic everyday life, put pressure on parents, and lead to worries. It can also be difficult for parents to know when to talk to their child about the seriousness of the situation.

In another study we conducted in a nursery setting, several parents talked about their challenges in assessing when to include their child, as they often hoped for the best while not wanting to upset their children (Lytje & Dyregrov, 2021). Sparing the children, however, rarely led to anything positive. The children were well aware that something was wrong, even if they did not know what, but could not process these feelings with the family. Thus, they were left to grieve alone, which negatively affected their well-being and ability to concentrate.

Whether children are aware of the seriousness of the illness or simply witness a family member's decline, the situation can result in changes in their behaviour. The fear of a relapse or the death of the ill person can cause many children to prioritize being at home over seeing friends and participating in leisure activities. This can erode social relationships and lead to friendships becoming weaker or even ending altogether. Other children may cope differently, choosing to spend as little time at home as possible as a means of escaping and 'forgetting' what is happening. This is particularly true in households with limited resources, where prior support may vanish entirely during the course of the illness. However, children who have been less present in the lead-up to a death may subsequently feel guilty about it.

One of the main issues during illness is that families often have to prioritize the needs of the ill person, which can leave other family members with less attention and support. This is due to the significant resources required to manage the illness, including medical appointments, hospitalizations, and the need for special care at home. Even resourceful families may struggle to give healthy children the same level of attention and support as before.

When the ill person is a parent, the family can be further strained. In addition to worries and extra care, the family may also experience the loss of a key contributor to daily tasks, care, and finances. In the case of sibling illness, healthy siblings may feel less loved as parents prioritize the needs and wishes of the ill child, leading to potential feelings of jealousy.

A particular problem during life-threatening illness is that it can be difficult for family members and children's institutions to keep track of what is happening in the home. In a previous study (Lytje, 2016a), a girl shared her experience with us:

> 'I think the teachers didn't really care, and neither did the pupils. They didn't know how serious it was. He was ill, but everybody gets ill at some point. Then when he died, there were just all of a sudden totally different reactions from teachers and pupils.'

The statement above describes the uncertainty that can arise among the child's entourage. It can be difficult to know exactly when an illness will become life-threatening.

Although many schools and nurseries have set procedures for what to do if someone dies, few have considered how to deal with life-threatening illness and when to take extra action. It is important for adults to have the courage to reach out to their families if they hear about an illness, especially if they are unsure about the seriousness of the situation. And even if the situation is not yet serious, but may become so, it is important to ensure that communication channels are in place so that the school or institution is informed if there are changes that may require additional focus and support for the child.

The idea of having to have such conversations can lead to fears of invading privacy, but our study (Lytje & Dyregrov, 2021) shows that families really appreciate it when professionals around the child take the lead and show genuine interest in ensuring the child's well-being.

Here are some recommendations for how to support children when they are faced with life-threatening illness in the family:

- Initiate contact as early as possible. Remember that more common illnesses can develop into critical ones.

- Establish open and effective communication channels with the child's family to stay informed about illness progression and any setbacks, as well as the overall well-being of the child and family.

- Be especially attentive and compassionate towards children who have seriously ill family members, as they may have fewer resources available to them. It is good to offer them support and care.

Sudden death

As discussed in Chapter 4 (The Impact of Loss on Children's Lives), research studies have indicated that children who experience the sudden death of a loved one are at a higher risk of facing health-related issues than other bereaved children (Dowdney, 2000; Lytje & Dyregrov, 2019). This is partly due to a decline in parental caregiving capacity during the period following the sudden death. In some countries, crisis help is activated after sudden deaths, which highlights the immediate upheaval experienced by the family. The family can struggle immensely with such losses and may not have the necessary resources to function normally.

When a child experiences the sudden death of a loved one due to suicide, murder, or accident, it is important to provide them with appropriate facts and support to help them understand what has happened and to be able to understand the adults' reactions. The parents may have been knocked sideways by the shock that has hit the family, and so the child will need good follow-up to help them cope with their grief.

Suicide and murder can be difficult (even taboo), topics, making it hard for support workers to navigate how much information to share and how to address the death in a child's environment, such as at school or in extracurricular activities. Often, parents choose to conceal the truth from their children and others outside the family, leading to confusion and a sense that something is being hidden. This can have a profound impact on the children, who may struggle to navigate school life without knowing what their classmates and friends know or think.

> After a teenager took her own life, the family received no guidance on how to address the death with others and was asked about what to say at school. They opted to keep the death private, but rumours began to circulate among the young people, leading to the situation worsening as talk turned to murder, accident, and the method of death. This not only caused distress for many pupils, but also made it difficult for the deceased teenager's siblings to navigate school life as they didn't know what their peers knew or thought. Effective crisis management, involving clear and honest communication between the police, school, and parents, could have helped prevent the spread of rumours and alleviated the situation for the young people.

If children are later told the truth, this can trigger anger towards those who concealed what happened, and lead to mistrust of the adults in the child's life.

If a family chooses to conceal the truth from outsiders after a sudden death, the child may feel burdened by the weight of the secret and inhibited in their ability to process their grief. In such cases, rumours can spread among acquaintances, leaving the child in a difficult position where they may isolate themselves from activities and fear what others may say or ask. As a support person, it is recommended to assist the child and family in telling the truth in a manner that protects their privacy while providing sufficient information to alleviate the child's anxiety about who knows what. Additionally, it may be helpful to provide guidance on how to approach difficult conversations.

Most sudden deaths have elements that can lead to trauma

reactions. It may be the way a child hears about the death, the child being in the accident themselves where one or more family members die, finding the dead person, or being present in the emergency room or intensive care unit at the time of death. This may lead to a mixture of post-traumatic reactions and grief that presents particular challenges and increases the importance of professional assistance.

After sudden deaths, particularly suicides, children can experience feelings of guilt and regret, often thinking 'If only I had done something differently...' If a child loses a parent, they may feel ashamed that they couldn't prevent the death or that they didn't express their love enough. In the case of a sibling's suicide, they may blame themselves for not recognizing the signs of distress. Additionally, children may carry the burden of a 'secret', knowing that the deceased had suicidal thoughts and feeling that they could have done more to prevent the tragedy (K. Dyregrov & A. Dyregrov, 2005). It's important to be aware of these possible reactions and to provide appropriate support for children who may be struggling with these difficult feelings.

Sudden deaths can also occur in larger accidents and disasters (see Chapter 12, Disasters, Terror, and Children's Grief). After such situations, it is often the adults who are updated on accident reports and so on. For the family, it may be important to record the information, as it can contribute to understanding and help answer possible questions that may arise as the child grows older. At the same time, children may continue to experience traumatic reminders through, for example, the media, which can negatively impact their grief processing.

Overall, this points to the importance of following families over time after sudden deaths and being particularly observant as to whether it is necessary to refer the child for additional help with post-traumatic problems.

Conclusion

As described in this chapter, losses can lead to different challenges. It is quite natural that jealousy is more likely to arise when parents spend all their time with an ill sibling, and that the management of daily tasks is more affected by the loss of a parent. While there are particular points to keep in mind in specific situations, the starting point should always be that each family is unique and has its own strengths and weaknesses. Families often react very differently to the same life experiences. Similarly, how families choose to cope with loss and the resilience of individual family members can vary greatly. In supporting a bereaved child, it is therefore essential to understand the family's starting point. This involves gaining insight, through dialogue, into what they think about the illness or death and how they are coping.

Chapter 6

Complicated Grief Processes

Introduction

Childhood losses are always difficult and affect children in virtually every area of their lives. Yet some losses occur in circumstances that further complicate a child's grieving process. In this chapter, we review the more complicated grief reactions children may experience in the aftermath of a death. While this knowledge is relevant to all readers, it is particularly important background knowledge for professionals who encounter children in their work. The purpose of this chapter is to provide you with a stronger understanding of how complicated grief reactions occur in children and when grief may become so demanding that it requires therapeutic intervention.

During the past decade, a significant amount of research has been dedicated to understanding situations where loss can necessitate professional intervention. This effort has led to the recognition of prolonged grief disorder (PGD) in the *International Classification of Diseases, version 11* (*ICD-11*) (World Health Organization, 2018) and a similar diagnosis in the fifth *Diagnostic and Statistical Manual of Mental Disorders* (*DSM-5-TR*) (American Psychiatric Association, 2022). For the first time in history, grief is acknowledged as something that can develop into a disorder. However, cautionary statements in the descriptive texts of these diagnoses indicate that more research is needed to support the inclusion of children (0–18 years old). It is possible that other forms of complicated grief in children also warrant research interest.

To determine whether a bereaved adult is suffering from PGD, inventories such as Prolonged Grief Disorder 13 have been created, and for children, similar inventories exist. However, these inventories tend to overlook the unique situation of a child grieving a loss. Children are heavily reliant on their social surroundings to make sense of what has happened and to cope with their loss. Their experience of loss is significantly influenced by the support and reactions of their parents and caregivers, the surrounding community, and society as a whole (e.g., wider family, friends, school, nursery). Studies (Luecken *et al.*, 2009; Worden, 1996) have shown that such influences are highly significant in predicting how well a child will cope following a loss. Therefore, there is a risk that in establishing a grief diagnosis for children, the research community may oversimplify children's grief by transferring adult models of thinking to their conceptualization of grief in children.

In a small study examining what 39 highly experienced clinicians and researchers from different parts of the world understood by 'complicated grief', many were found to have significant difficulty defining the term (A. Dyregrov & K. Dyregrov, 2013). Respondents agreed that what primarily distinguishes normal grief from complicated grief is intensity and duration, as well as the fact that grief reactions seem fixed or rigid. We know that many young people push reactions away, mostly because of their strength. When this becomes so prominent that it causes loss of normal functioning, it indicates that they are struggling with their grief and need adult help.

We therefore use the term 'complicated grief' to refer to children and young people who do not return to normal functioning over time in terms of contact with friends or in performance at school. In complicated grief, changes in life and in the family are not mastered and normal developmental tasks (becoming independent, learning to regulate emotions, interacting with others, etc.) are disrupted and delayed. Even with the knowledge we have today, it is difficult to draw a clear line between what is 'normal grief' and what should be considered complicated grief when a child loses a parent or sibling.

In this chapter, we review various forms of complicated grief reactions that children may experience in the aftermath of a loss.

Different forms of complicated grief in children

While prolonged grief is the most common complicated grief among adults, we find that children and adolescents can develop other complications. To date, however, these have not been widely studied and their prevalence is therefore unknown. Prolonged grief is not a new phenomenon in the research world. As early as 1963, John Bowlby described different types of complicated grief in children under the term 'pathological mourning' (A. Dyregrov & K. Dyregrov, 2012).

Bowlby (1963) believed that the complications could be grouped into the following forms:

- persistent and unconscious yearning for the return of the one who has been lost

- intense and persistent anger and reproach expressed towards various objects, including oneself

- absorption in caring for someone else who has also been bereaved, amounting to compulsion

- denial that the deceased is permanently lost, i.e., absence of grief (here the death is not acknowledged, but Bowlby accepts that there is some awareness of it).

The forms, according to Bowlby, were not mutually exclusive and could exist in different combinations with other mental health problems. He considered restoration of normal functions as characteristic of ordinary grief or healthy mourning, while remaining preoccupied with the deceased in thought and action characterized complicated grief, or 'pathological mourning' as Bowlby terms it. In a 1996 study, Worden followed, over time, a large group of children who had lost parents. He describes similar forms of complicated grief to Bowlby, but adds a form characterized by children's reactions that manifest as physical complaints, such as headaches, stomach aches, or the like.

The understanding of the meaning of trauma is more recent and not covered by Bowlby's categories. Children's grief reactions may be complicated by the circumstances of the death or by situations during the course of an illness. Psychiatrist Robert Pynoos (1992) discusses how traumatic circumstances complicate grief processing because they require many of a child's resources, and processing the trauma effects takes precedence over grieving. Grief with strong trauma elements is often called 'traumatic grief'. Whether this should be described as a type of complicated grief or rather as post-traumatic stress reactions is debatable. In any case, it is important to know whether or in what way traumatic elements complicate grief. Children do not need to be present to experience a death as traumatic – they can create their own fantasies about what happened. This is illustrated by the following example:

> Following the suicide of her father, an 11-year-old girl experienced intense and recurrent fantasies about the event, which were complicating her grieving process. Despite not being present at the time of her father's death, she had vivid mental fantasies of how it occurred. After several weeks, she was referred to a psychologist for support. To address her distressing thoughts, the psychologist arranged a conversation with the person who found her father, to provide the girl with facts about what occurred. The therapist also taught her techniques to modify her fantasies, such as re-scripting and mental editing, in which she imagined editing the 'film' in her mind. These methods were aimed to disrupt the storage of the distressing fantasy and reduce the emotional intensity of the images she had formed.

In our clinical practice, it has become apparent that children often develop complicated grief reactions due to the ways in which death is managed within the family context. These reactions may be reflective of inadequate family interactions, such as adults not providing children with sufficient information regarding the circumstances of the death, leading to misunderstandings. Children may also incorrectly blame themselves for the loss, and if their perceptions are not corrected by adults, this can further exacerbate their grief. Additionally, if a surviving parent is grappling with their own grief to such an extent that it impacts their parenting capacity, it can impede a normal grieving process for the child. Poor communication in the family, the presence of family secrets, or a lack of dialogue about the death may also contribute to complicated grief in children over time. In particular, weakened parenting capacity can prevent parents from effectively assisting their child in regulating their emotions, which is important for coping with the loss in the long term.

> Following the sudden death of their mother, the father of a teenage daughter and an adult young daughter struggled to adjust to his new role as the main caregiver. The girls expressed frustration that their father did not show them the same level of care and support that their mother had; for example, they had to ask him to send encouraging text messages before exams and keep up with how they were doing. In family conversations, they accused him of not caring enough and hiding his emotions, leading to feelings of hopelessness. The father was overwhelmed by grief and found it challenging to express his love for his daughters in a meaningful way, which further complicated the family climate and reinforced the daughters' longing for their mother.

There is one type of complicated grief that is more prominent in children than in adults, and that is grief repression. This reaction is particularly prominent in adolescents. Both adults and children may find that emotions are immediately kept at bay after being told of a death, but children and young people frequently continue to use repression and avoidance as a defence against the strong and difficult emotions triggered by the loss. It is often very difficult to know when this regulation is appropriate and good, and when it becomes part of a pattern that should cause concern. Younger children can go in and out of grief quickly, a characteristic that can sometimes startle those around them. At the same time, young people may keep grief at bay for longer periods of time without it becoming something that requires treatment. It is not an easy task to know when suppression is appropriate and when it should lead to professional follow-up.

Professionals may be contacted by parents who are concerned about a child's lack of grief response after losing a parent or a sibling. They can feel that the child talks too little about the dead person. However, this may be due to a persistent shock reaction that protects and prevents the child from fully taking in the situation. This is where you can look at how the child is functioning over time to assess whether they need further help.

An 11-year-old boy was referred by the family doctor on the mother's persistent recommendation because he had showed no reaction after his father's death from cancer and because he did not want to talk about the father. Three months had passed since the death. The boy had never been one to talk much about emotions. When asked directly whether he struggled with any intrusive memories from the illness or the death, he replied in the negative (which means no sign of post-traumatic stress disorder). He was doing well at school, had an understanding contact teacher, and his mother was in good contact with the school, who reported that schoolwork was going well. Both mother and school reported that he sought out friends as before and continued his interest in football, and the mother did not feel he had changed much since the death.

In this case, the parent appeared to be overly concerned despite the child functioning well. While there may be potential issues in the future, preventive therapy is challenging. Therefore, it is good for therapists to assess for any functional deficits. If there are none, the child may not be motivated for follow-up.

However, prolonged reactions can lead to functional impairment that requires therapeutic intervention. Clinically, we have seen that adolescents in particular may have few or no reactions, neither post-traumatic disorders nor a strong sense of loss, but then they may have great difficulty learning at school. It is reasonable to believe that young people spend considerable cognitive resources on keeping grief at bay, without even realizing it, and that this weakens their ability to learn at school. In a therapeutic context, the intervention here would be about motivating the young person to gradually approach the loss in a controlled way, so that cognitive resources can be released. This is a difficult task because the very suppression allows them to feel relatively good while the therapist wants them to go into something that involves emotional pain.

A related variant of complicated grief is characterized by avoidance. Here, children don't want to talk about the deceased, and they try to avoid activities or places they associate with them. The avoidance pattern can be more extensive, for example avoiding TV programmes that mention deaths (e.g., crime shows) or any particular food that they associate with the deceased. This can limit both the child's and the family's daily life. Children may also isolate themselves from activities outside the home to guard against reminders. While adults can see and understand that something needs to be done about this, it is more difficult for children who have less life experience and less developed emotional control to be motivated to open up and talk.

Children can develop a complicated grief in which a particular emotional response becomes dominant. It may be anger, guilt, or worry and anxiety. It can also be a mixture of these, reinforced by poor communication in the family. This is illustrated by the following example:

> A three-year-old boy developed a strong aversion to his mother after the death of his sister. The mother had taken his sister to the hospital, where she died soon after. The boy was not given an explanation about why his sister died and he developed a fear that his mother would also take him away and he would be the next victim. Consequently, he became terrified of his mother and did not want to have anything to do with her, preferring only to be with his father.

Understanding children's thinking and the context of their experiences is crucial to understanding their fears and reactions. One common reaction in children is a strong concern for the well-being of other family members after a loss. Despite its prevalence, this reaction has not been extensively researched. Especially if children have lost a parent, the fear of losing the other parent as well can be very pronounced. It is difficult to say where to draw the line between normal and inappropriate anxiety, but when separation anxiety (which is of course common in children of pre-school and early school age) means that they will not let their parent out of their sight, it becomes problematic. Sometimes such fears are stimulated by misinformation or misinterpretation of information. Children may hear adults say of one grandparent that he or she 'fell asleep', and subsequently be afraid that this will happen to others they care about, or themselves.

A child's fear of suffering from the same illness as the deceased can become so overwhelming that it affects their ability to function in everyday life. For example, a nine-year-old boy spent much of his time feeling for tumours growing inside him after his father died of a brain tumour. He felt that he could literally feel lumps growing on his forehead. Without early intervention, a long-lasting fear of the disease can develop. Lack of understanding about the disease and the body, such as believing that cancer is contagious, can make children even more vulnerable to these fears.

While some level of guilt and self-blame soon after a death is common and often disappears with the help of good adult care, in some cases these reactions can persist and go unnoticed by adults. Here is an example of this:

> A 14-year-old girl sought help from a psychologist due to her ongoing conflicts with her teachers. During the conversation with the psychologist, it became apparent that she had been struggling with intense feelings of guilt since her two-year-old sister died of a critical illness three years before. The girl believed that she was responsible for her sister's death because she took her on a ride in her baby-stroller in cold weather on the day the illness started. The overwhelming guilt had been affecting her academic performance and relationships with others. The girl had not shared her thoughts with any adult, and the psychologist was able to help her process her emotions and thoughts to overcome the guilt.

When anger develops after the death, it often leads to early contact with support services. The anger may be directed at someone who did not 'prevent' the death, say, against a parent who took his or her own life, with statements like 'Dad is an idiot who killed himself.' This anger can lead to conflicts with parents, siblings, classmates, or teachers at school. In such cases, parents may seek advice on how to communicate about the loss within the family and how to seek appropriate treatment. These conversations can provide a safe space for the child to talk about what the loss has meant and may help to avoid conflicts that might cause difficulties for the child.

In some cases, children who experience the death of a loved one may develop distressing physical ailments because of suppressing their grief and not expressing their emotions. This can manifest as stomach problems, muscle or skeletal pain, headaches, and other physical symptoms that divert attention away from the underlying grief. In some cases, if the physical symptoms are similar to those of the deceased, this might be caused by anxiety where their fear and imagination have initiated the symptoms. Furthermore, some children may regulate their physical tensions after death with self-harm, while others may develop eating disorders (Bylund-Grenklo *et al.*, 2014). To prevent these complications, it is important to initiate necessary support services early on.

The prevalence of complicated grief

The prevalence of complicated grief in children is still largely unknown due to a lack of consensus on its definition and limited measurement tools. Among the various types of complicated grief, prolonged grief has been the most extensively studied. Melhem and colleagues (2011) found that 10% of children who had lost a parent between the ages of 8 and 17 still experienced persistent and intense grief reactions almost three years after the loss. Spuij and co-workers (2012) identified that prolonged grief is distinguishable from grief-related depression and PTSD in children, but did not report on its prevalence. Another study by Boelen and colleagues (2017) identified three subgroups of children who experienced the loss of a close family member: a resilient group, a group with prolonged grief reactions, and a group who experienced both prolonged grief and post-traumatic reactions.

While the number of children with prolonged grief is often used to estimate the prevalence of complicated grief, it is important to note that other forms of complicated grief also exist. As such, the actual percentage of children struggling with complicated reactions may be much higher than that reported by Melhem and colleagues (2011). Further research is needed to better understand the prevalence of different forms of complicated grief in children. A nationwide study in Sweden by Bylund-Grenklo and co-workers (2016) found that nearly half of young adults who lost a parent to cancer between the ages of 13 and 16 still reported unprocessed grief six to nine years later, indicating the need for continued research and support for grieving children.

What constitutes a risk of complicated grief?

We have previously described how past trauma and loss, including exposure to violence and abuse, increase the risk of problems during bereavement (A. Dyregrov & K. Dyregrov, 2016). Moreover, the risk factors present when the illness and loss occur – such as exposure to traumatic moments and exposure to danger – may contribute to a skewed development. The family's financial situation, moving, changing schools, and lack of help and support are other factors that can increase the risk of complicated grief.

Children rely on parents and other adults for information, to help them understand their loss, and to care for them in a good and nurturing way. If information is limited or children cannot talk freely with the surviving parent about what has happened or about their experience, this increases the risk of long-lasting problems (Tremblay & Israel, 1998). Lack of life experience also means an increased risk of misunderstanding facts or misinterpreting adult reactions. In a study we conducted on parental death from cancer, we found that lack of information after a parent's death made children's grief processing more problematic (K. Dyregrov & A. Dyregrov, 2011).

Bylund-Grenklo and colleagues (2013) demonstrated that facts provided by physicians to adolescents aged 13–16 years about illness, treatment, and death prior to a parent's death resulted in a reduced risk of depressive symptoms six to nine years after death. Good information was further associated with significantly greater confidence in the medical treatment the parents received.

The atmosphere or climate that parents or a surviving parent manage to create can be both a protective factor and a risk factor in the period after a death. A warm climate, where rules about home time, sleeping time, and so on are maintained, is protective for children who have lost a parent (Lin *et al.*, 2004; Shapiro *et al.*, 2014). And vice versa: lack of parental care increases the risk of developing mental health problems (Kranzler *et al.*, 1990; Luecken, 2008; Tremblay & Israel, 1998). Although it has not been extensively studied, our clinical experience and specific studies suggest that if a parent enters a new relationship shortly following the loss of a partner (especially if it is the mother who dies), this can create problems in bereaved children, especially adolescent girls (Riches & Dawson, 2000).

It can be difficult for a parent who loses a partner, or for parents who lose a child, to talk to their children about the deceased because it can arouse their own feelings of loss and longing. Although there are few studies, our clinical experience is that complicated grief in adults makes openness at home difficult and thus increases the risk of children being left alone to grieve. This was also concluded in a study by Shapiro and colleagues (2014) on children who had lost their fathers. The researchers highlighted the importance of the surviving parent's way of coping with the loss and found that mothers' communication patterns, rather than those of the child, were important in how the child coped.

Children need to develop or maintain an internal relationship with the one they have lost, where they do not hold the deceased too close, but also do not push them away completely. Conversations that allow this are called 'elaborative conversations' and are considered important in children's development. If, for various reasons, the surviving parent 'neglects' such conversations, it complicates the child's grieving process. Children depend on parents to learn to recognize, express, and regulate their emotions, and if the parenting capacity of the surviving parent weakens over time, this can have consequences for the child's later well-being. It is also clear that children are at greater risk of long-term problems if they have previously experienced bereavement or have had mental health problems in the past (Worden, 1996).

There is some evidence that sudden deaths generally cause more problems than expected deaths, but this is not clear-cut, and the strain of long-term illness can take its toll on everyone in a family. The negative impact of a sudden death is thought to be linked to a lack of preparation and the fact that children may be present at the time of death, with all the trauma this entails. But long-term illness can also have trauma elements associated with critical situations that arise, for example if children witness major physical changes in the seriously ill or dying person. Exposure to strong, potentially traumatizing situations associated with illness and death can produce subsequent trauma symptoms (Kaplow *et al.*, 2014).

Few studies have examined the impact of children's social networks on their risk of developing subsequent problems, but we know from clinical work that children who have understanding friends and adults they can turn to for support cope better with the situation than those who feel alone with their grief. We have shown in a small study (K. Dyregrov & A. Dyregrov, 2011) that children can become insecure in interpersonal relationships and afraid to attach to anyone for fear of losing them again. They may then withdraw from social life and become lonelier in their grief. In general, however, we can say that lack of social support from friends, family, or school is associated with several problems (K. Dyregrov & A. Dyregrov, 2008).

When does grief require therapeutic intervention?

We have described above how in many cases death involves children experiencing a situation that can cause traumatic after-effects. If such reactions persist beyond the first weeks and are highly distressing for the child, there is no reason to wait before seeking help. This avoids the effects of trauma blocking more normal grief reactions. In the area of post-trauma, there are simple mapping instruments that can be used.[1] More information on

---

1   For example, www.childrenandwar.org/projectsresources/measures or www. global-psychotrauma.net/grief.

assessment tools for grief in children can be found in the article by Ennis and colleagues (2022).

Yearning and longing are normal grief reactions and do not require professional intervention. If parents or others in contact with the child are concerned, a good tip is to talk to a psychologist or other professional and get advice on what can be done.

Therapeutic interventions may need to be considered if the child:

- withdraws from friends and adults

- changes their behaviour dramatically and persistently

- develops phobic reactions that persist over time

- displays strong repressed emotions related to the loss

- talks about self-harm or suicide

- experiences strong feelings of self-blame and guilt

- has violent or disturbing thoughts related to the loss.

Conclusion

This chapter has emphasized the importance of recognizing and addressing complicated grief in children. By understanding the various ways in which complicated grief can present itself, parents, schools, and professionals can provide the support and guidance necessary for the child's well-being and development. It is important to tailor the approach to each individual child, taking into account their unique experiences and needs. Fortunately, there are established and effective treatment methods available for children with complex grief. In Chapter 11, Therapy with Children, we will delve deeper into the various interventions and treatments that can help children cope with and overcome complicated grief, allowing them to thrive and lead fulfilling lives.

Chapter 7

Coping with Loss

Introduction

Childhood loss can have a profound impact on children, leaving them with the daunting task of grappling with grief and navigating through a sea of painful emotions. Yet, amid the sorrow, it is important to acknowledge that children possess an innate desire to find their way back to a sense of normalcy in their lives. While they may never forget the person they lost, they long for the opportunity to continue living, to return to school, to spend time with friends, and to have hope for the future. Achieving this balance between honouring the memory of the deceased and moving forward requires a degree of mastery over grief, which is the focus of this chapter. Through exploring the different ways in which children cope with and master their grief, this chapter aims to equip readers with valuable knowledge and insight. It is important to note that the path to such skill is unique for each child, shaped by their individual experiences of loss.

What is coping?

Coping is not an easy concept to define, but we choose here to let coping cover what a child does in thought, action, and emotion to cope with the loss they have suffered. This includes the thinking and action strategies the child uses, how they manage to use their family and friends when facing dark moments, what they do to cope with the situation, and how flexible they are in their thoughts and actions when facing the new life circumstances. Coping means using internal resources (experiences, thoughts, and abilities to express and regulate emotions) and external resources (family, friends, social network, and professional help) to live as well as possible after a loss. All coping happens in interaction with others, and good coping is about allowing others to support and help so that the loss does not impair the child's ability to function over time.

There is no single form of coping that is better than others. What children do to cope with loss must be adapted to what they are struggling with, their past experience, how long it has been since the loss, and the support available to them. It is important both that children can vary what they do and how they think, and that they can regulate emotions in response to changing circumstances. In a study of adults, Gupta and Bonanno (2011) demonstrated that individuals struggling with complicated grief have problems with flexibly increasing or decreasing their expression of emotions relative to other grievers. Clinically we observe that children and adolescents struggle with emotional regulation and may be extra challenged to respond in a flexible manner.

Distancing oneself from intense emotional pain and grief can be necessary and beneficial if the situation is almost unbearable. It can prevent a child from becoming completely overwhelmed. The use of distancing, which allows a pause before the child then later dares to approach the loss, can reflect expressive flexibility in coping here. There is also research to suggest this is effective (Wolchik *et al.*, 2008). However, overusing the distancing forms of coping (e.g., avoiding anything that reminds one of the deceased) often cause problems.

The capacity for flexible coping is important because it enables children to adapt what they do or think to a situation that changes over time. What may be helpful early after the loss – during the shock that displaces the emotional reality – is not so appropriate if it is the only method children use through their grieving process. Children need to open up and deal with their feelings, not just close them off. In many respects, our thinking follows Bonanno's (2021) flexibility sequence for self-regulation: starting with *context sensitivity* where what is done matches the demands of the situation; following with the choice of method from a *repertoire*; and ending with *feedback monitoring*, where a method is checked for whether it works or not. Children may lack a broad repertoire of coping methods and must rely on parents or professionals to be taught tools to deal with the situation.

There are many different coping methods to deal with the loss of a loved one. Children may avoid or push away all thoughts and feelings, seek support from and talk to others, distract themselves with activities, listen to music, exercise, gather information about the deceased, use wishful thinking, and so on. It is common to distinguish between emotion-focused and problem-focused coping, and between avoidance-oriented and approach-oriented coping. Research shows that using one of these methods alone does not always provide the best approach. It varies with the problems and the time after the loss, and children tend to use parts of all these coping methods (Krattenmacher *et al.*, 2013). Although differences in the strength of boys' and girls' responses have been uncovered, this has been studied to a much lesser extent compared to differences in coping strategies. Our clinical experience is that girls are more likely than boys to find someone to talk to, while boys refrain more from approaching painful thoughts or emotions (more avoidance-oriented).

In relation to adults, Stroebe and Schuts' (1999) two-track model of grief has become the predominant way of understanding people's grief process. It divides into loss-oriented coping and restoration-oriented coping. Good coping involves finding a balance between these two tracks, that is, alternating between the methods over time. However, few studies have examined whether this model is as appropriate for children's coping as it is for adults'. Our clinical experience is that children often use 'walk away' strategies to a greater extent than adults because their ability to regulate strong emotions is more limited. At the same time, they also alternate between approaching and walking away (avoidance) over time. With age and maturation, children often return to their losses and have to re-master the thoughts and feelings that their expanded insight into what happened brings. We find that children also do this best when they can find a balance between loss-oriented and restoration-oriented coping.

Children's development of coping strategies

Children do not come into the world equipped with good coping mechanisms, but with a huge number of neurons in the brain that develop, strengthen, and network with each other through inter-actions with parents and other carers. Personal resources are not developed in isolation, but in interaction with the experiences a child has in the social and cultural context in which they grow up. Children are endowed with different personality traits and temper-aments, which require timely and appropriate feedback from the environment in order for them to regulate their emotions and adapt their responses to the adversities they encounter. The connectivity of neurons and networks is influenced by the 'climate' in which a person lives during their childhood years. If parents are deeply affected by their own grief or are struggling with other problems in their lives that go beyond their ability to meet their children's needs, children's ability to regulate emotions and cope with adversity may be impaired.

A child's ability to regulate emotions is important as a frame-work for coping. When children are newborns, their parents help them regulate the body's functions – feeding them when they need it, washing and grooming them, and stimulating their senses in different ways. Gradually, children develop the ability to regulate their needs, whether for food, to engage in activities, or to satisfy

their curiosity. We rarely think about the fact that children are constantly increasing their ability to up- and down-regulate anxiety
and excitement. We see it when they explore the environment and
move away from their base of safety (the parents), only to return
to the safe place if they get too far away. Gradually, they learn to
extend boundaries under the safe eye contact of parents, who are
paying attention to them. During this stage, a period of prolonged
impairment of parental capacity to assist in this development may
result in a reduced capacity for emotion regulation and impaired
coping flexibility.

Knowing the important role parents play in children's emotional
development, it stands to reason that helping parents who lose a
partner or child will be of great importance. This may mean that
parents are available to help children when they experience strong
emotions triggered by a death, and can contribute to children's
development and emotion regulation. Indeed, this is emphasized
both theoretically (Hajal & Paley, 2020) and in clinical studies of
children and bereavement (Sandler *et al.*, 2018). Without the ability
to regulate emotions, coping with grief becomes difficult.

Our ability to later connect with other people is also deeply
dependent on interactions with our close environment. The degree
of stability in contact with adults around us during childhood has
an impact on our ability to cope with losses that affect us during
childhood, adolescence, and adulthood. If adults are unstable or
only slightly available, this can lead to various kinds of difficulties
with later attachment (Granqvist *et al.*, 2017).

Studies of children's coping strategies

Hogan and DeSantis (1994) examined what 140 adolescents
between the ages of 13 and 18 thought helped or hindered their
coping after the loss of a sister or brother. They found three factors
that helped them cope with the loss:

1. Personal factors such as stress-reducing activities, for example playing an instrument, keeping busy, or letting go of built-up tension by shouting and crying. They could also cope with the loss through personal faith or inner strength.

2. Support from family and parents who were there for them and helped them accept their feelings as normal, and shared memories of the deceased with them. Other relatives and friends also helped them to cope by being there for them when they needed it.

3. Professional help from health services and religious institutions, and participation in bereavement groups.

Among the conditions in the children themselves that Hogan and DeSantis (1994) found hindered or made coping difficult were: strong, painful reactions consisting of intrusive thoughts and feelings such as guilt and shame; loneliness; distressing images and memories; and not wanting to realize that the loss of the deceased was final. Also, the social environment made coping difficult when the children experienced lack of sensitivity as well as rumours and gossip from their surroundings.

Lövgren and colleagues (2019) studied 174 adolescents and young adults who had lost siblings to cancer in Sweden and found that siblings described four different ways of coping:

1. They thought about their dead sibling and acknowledged and expressed their feelings.

2. They distracted or occupied themselves.

3. They engaged in spiritual or religious beliefs/activities (e.g., believing in meeting the sibling again).

4. They waited for time to pass, having patience to use time as a healer.

With the exception of waiting for time to pass, these ways of coping were associated with having worked through their grief to a greater extent than those who did not use such methods.

In a study we participated in, we found that adults who had experienced loss in childhood and reported good family support used four inappropriate ways of coping (abuse, withdrawal, self-recrimination, and emotional eating) significantly less than other bereaved people (Høeg et al., 2017).

The importance of access to facts on children's coping

Both before and after deaths from illness and unexpected deaths, children's understanding of what has been happening is an important foundation for their later coping. Without coherence and structure in the sequence of events, it is difficult to get a grip on what has happened. The smaller a child is when illness and death strike, the more dependent they are on adults for information. At the same time, adults often withhold information for various reasons, most often because they do not think children are old or mature enough to understand, or because they fear that the facts will make the loss even more difficult for them. Unfortunately, this often causes additional difficulties for children in the form of a limited understanding of what has happened, fantasies that are worse than reality, or misunderstandings that can negatively affect their inner thoughts. Although the idea of shielding children is a good one, and may work in the short term, it is usually associated with weakened trust in adults over time, and more problems in coping. The research is therefore relatively unambiguous: it is best to be open and honest and share most of the factual information with children (but not necessarily all of the details) (Ellis et al., 2013; Martinčeková et al., 2020; Schepers, 2019; Sheehan et al., 2019).

An avoidant coping style

We have already mentioned that children who cut themselves off from anything that reminds them of the deceased use an avoidant mastery style; this is most prominent among adolescents (12 years and older). It is difficult to distinguish between when an avoidant coping style works constructively for children and helps them to function despite the loss, and when the child has to expend so much mental energy keeping thoughts at bay that they do not have enough resources to maintain daily functioning. We assume that the ability to 'switch off' from the loss at times is an important coping resource that allows children to maintain social contact with the environment, normal schooling, and participation in leisure activities as before. It is only when over time children push aside all reactions and thoughts associated with the loss that it can come into conflict with daily functioning.

A 14-year-old girl lived with a mother who had life-threatening cancer that was spreading. The girl did not want updates about her mother's illness. The family was worried about her because she had started to withdraw from her friends. In talks with a psychologist, she said she would rather not know about the illness because it made her anxious. She had been told by a classmate that her mother's cancer had spread. The friend had heard her mother talking about it in a phone conversation. The girl spoke of extensive avoidance of things, including not being able to look at a sofa that was right inside the door of their home – a couch the mother often lay on when she was fatigued from disease or treatment. Seeing it reminded her that her mother was ill. In this case, it was obvious that avoidance had begun to affect the girl's daily life and that together with the psychologist she needed to work on developing a more active and confrontational coping style.

Accepting help and advice from others when needed is a sign of good coping. Avoidance strategies create barriers to this. Children who do not want to talk about the loss, or who refuse to see a health visitor or to spend an hour with a psychologist, will not benefit from the help of others. This cannot be blamed on the child, but it means that we adults must try to break down the barriers that prevent them from receiving help. Professionals need to offer help in a way that the child can benefit from, which requires that the carer has skills to mediate and motivate.

It also requires a willingness on the part of the child to listen and to be positive about the advice or methods presented and through the contact develop the ability and patience to approach their loss. Barriers to receiving help may be created by parents if they do not think it will help for their child to talk to someone other than themselves. Barriers can also arise in the external support services, for example when the child first faces many questionnaires or lengthy diagnostic sessions or can only get help after a long time on a waiting list. There can therefore be many reasons why a child may not want to open up about a loss, but it is always the adults' responsibility to make it as easy as possible for the child to talk about it.

An active and confrontational coping style

Seeking knowledge can be a way of coping with loss. When children repeatedly ask questions about a death, they gradually build up more knowledge about what happened, which can lead to a better understanding of the loss. Without reliable facts, children may be frightened by their own fantasies and thoughts. Information that helps children create a timeline and interpret their own and others' reactions can help them better cope with their grief (A. Dyregrov & Kristensen, 2020).

Participating in rituals can be a helpful way for a child to confront the loss and come to accept the new reality. Seeing the deceased and attending the funeral or memorial service can make the abstract concept of death more concrete and help children avoid later fantasies that the deceased is still alive. Engaging in conversations with emergency personnel or witnesses to an accident, visiting the scene of the accident, or going to a hospital ward can also contribute to the child's understanding and coping over time, even if it is initially painful. In addition, this confrontational approach may involve viewing pictures, videos, or other possessions associated with the deceased. Although it can be difficult at first, the pain is gradually dulled through this process, while avoidance can require mental energy over time.

Research has shown that expressive strategies, where children are encouraged to verbalize their emotions, are associated with better coping and overall well-being (Howell *et al.*, 2016). When children feel comfortable sharing their inner experiences and feelings, it often leads to greater support and empathy from others, which can help to reduce feelings of intense longing and grief. It is important to create an understanding and supportive environment for children to express their grief. While initially, outgoing children may receive more social support, it is important to note that all children can benefit from learning different expressive strategies to enhance their coping skills.

Expressing emotions is not limited to conversations and words alone. Physical exercise, play, artistic activities, writing, and music can also serve as effective mediums for expression. It's worth noting that one of the most effective follow-up interventions for grieving children is music therapy groups (Hilliard, 2007). Different forms of expression can be organized in family and intervention settings to help children cope with the loss of a loved one. Furthermore, the family's attitude towards the child's coping is important. Research has shown that 'positive parenting' is particularly important after parental loss, including creating a warm and nurturing environment while expecting rules to be followed (Haine *et al.*, 2006; Lin *et al.*, 2004). Chapter 11, Therapy with Children, elaborates further on this topic.

Exercise and leisure activities can also contribute to coping. However, such activities can be both positive and negative: negative, because many of these activities may produce a sense of missing a deceased parent, sibling, or friend who was often with the child during the activity; positive, because children can quickly become engrossed in what they are doing, and the activity becomes a good break from grief. Many children find that exercise and leisure activities improve their mood and counteract passivity and depression.

It is important to note that even children who are initially expressive and able to talk about their thoughts and feelings after a death may experience reactions from their environment that cause them to shut down. For openness to be effective, those to whom children are open must also be open and supportive. If children sense that their parents will be upset when they ask about the loss, they may avoid the subject to protect them. Additionally, friends may show that they now need to 'get over it' relatively soon after the loss, or children may feel pressure not to talk about the deceased. Interactions with the social environment can be complicated, and research has shown that social support can both facilitate and prevent coping with grief (Hogan & DeSantis, 1994).

If a child does not want information about what has happened to be mentioned at school, this sends signals that make openness difficult and may discourage others from making contact. The child may not understand that, while this can make it easier to return to school in the short term, it may hamper communication with friends in the longer term. Concrete examples of how openness can make everyday life easier can help children to cope better.

A young girl who had lost her father before starting secondary school initially didn't want anyone at school to know, despite some of her friends already being aware. Through the conversation with a psychologist, it became apparent that she tended to use an avoidant coping style. The psychologist shared some stories about other young people her age who had been in a similar situation and had chosen a more open approach. This led to a more open discussion, and the psychologist suggested that the girl considered the implications of not giving everyone the same information, and how then knowing who and what others knew could be difficult. By the next session, the girl had changed her mind and said, 'I think what you said last time about school was wise.'

Clearly communicating your needs and desires for support to others is an active form of coping that can facilitate your social network's ability to provide support. This coping style is typically not present until adolescence, but young people who are able to express their needs can help those around them know how to help. This is important because children and young people may lack experience with grief and may be hesitant to offer support for fear of making things worse or because they feel socially awkward. Teachers and parents of friends can offer advice to those supporting a grieving friend to ensure that their support is effective.

Coping by seeing things in a new perspective

While younger children make little use of thinking skills and mental control to cope with death, this is seen more in adolescents. The following example may exemplify this.

Lesley was 12 years old when her mother died. As an adult, she recalled that she received little help after it happened. She rowed out in a small boat, lay on her back in the boat, and wondered how she was going to get through it. 'I have to do it on my own. I have to have my mum in mind to help me, but I can't think about her too much, it'll be too hard,' she thought. Another thing she said to herself was: 'If I have children, I'll have to teach them to cope without me.' She had practised this when she had children. A new death that struck her as an adult prompted her to seek help, but she continued to both remember and use mental control as a way to cope with the new death.

Bereaved children talk about how they see themselves as more mature than their peers. They can see how something positive has come out of the tragic event. They now know how fleeting life is; they know how to support a friend who is struggling – or they know what is important in life and what matters little. This is a coping resource. They see the situation in perspective and reflect on their own situation but would of course rather have been spared such 'learning'.

We have discussed how decisions, ways of thinking, and mental control are used by adults (K. Dyregrov *et al.*, 2016). This has not been studied in children; but in encounters with young clients approaching adulthood, we recognize this as a common coping strategy. They decide that the loss should have a positive meaning in their lives and that life should be lived on in a way that honours the deceased. Some use them as a motivation to make the best of their lives: 'She would have been proud of me if she could see me now.'

Coping through contact with others

In addition to conversation with others, there are other aspects of expressive coping that can aid in the grieving process. Interacting with others, whether it be parents, friends, or the wider community, can have its own inherent value. It allows for connection with people, provides present and future meaning, and aids in distancing and distracting oneself from grief. Adults often report feeling their best in everyday life when they are with others (Csikszentmihalyi, 1997). Similarly, children are social beings who derive affirmation and meaning from interactions with people. A supportive environment that recognizes their needs and provides social support can often facilitate children's coping.

Finding comfort in the company of others who have experienced a similar loss can also contribute to coping, and many children find this to be valuable, whether they meet other bereaved people individually or as part of a grief group. In such settings, children may not feel the need to explain everything as they intuitively understand each other's experiences. Although there are only a few methodologically robust studies to show the beneficial health effects of grief groups (Bergman *et al.*, 2017), pre- to post-assessment studies indicate increases in perceived social support and reduced grief symptomatology (i.e., Linder *et al.*, 2022).

While research on the impact of bereavement groups on health measures has been inconclusive, many children and young people find participation beneficial. They often express appreciation for hearing that others react in the same way they do, and feel reassured that their emotions are normal. Grief groups can vary in structure, frequency, duration, leadership, and format (open or closed, with or without fixed topics).

Coping through self-help

Children have access to various self-help strategies to cope with loss, including writing about the loss, engaging in rituals, or setting aside specific times to think about the deceased (such as before bedtime). These strategies may be learned from parents, the internet, healthcare professionals, or a bereavement group. These methods can be useful for children to deal with specific difficulties in everyday life. For instance, if a child has trouble falling asleep due to intrusive thoughts, setting aside time during the day to address these thoughts and redirecting attention to a distracting activity, such as counting backward from 1000 in fives or sevens, may help the child fall asleep more quickly.

Worries about others in the family are common among troubled children and adolescents. This takes a lot of energy and can impair their ability to concentrate at school. Teaching them ways to better control their worries can therefore be a good way to help them.

One method that can be used both for this and by those who spend too much of the time experiencing longing is to postpone worrying or worrying to a period of 15–20 minutes at a certain time of day. If these are worries they are struggling with, children can call this their 'Worry Time'. If it's missing a mum or dad that keeps coming to mind, they can call it 'Mum Time' or 'Dad Time'. Their task is then to go 'close' to the thoughts during this time but otherwise postpone them until this appointed time, each time they appear. This is a method that is very useful for many people to better control thoughts that are otherwise stressful when they intrude frequently.

There are also self-help methods to enable individuals to better manage intrusive memories, reduce feelings of guilt, and alleviate self-recrimination. More information about these methods can be found in our previous work (A. Dyregrov, 2010).

Conclusion

It is imperative to emphasize the importance of seeking out the child's perspective by asking, 'What specifically is most difficult for you right now?' Once the challenge is identified, it is essential to choose a method that directly addresses the child's concerns. Although some responses may not have a prescribed method of addressing them, such as when a child states that life feels meaningless, the adult must work together with them to find a reason to look forward to the future and build an understanding that their current situation is temporary. Children process loss differently, and it is our responsibility both to steer them away from approaches that we know from experience and research are linked to long-term issues, and to supplement these with constructive strategies when necessary.

Chapter 8

Grief in the Family

Introduction: The effects of death on family dynamics and coping strategies

The impact of death on a family can vary depending on who has passed away. For instance, if a child loses a sibling, it means not only that the child has lost a sibling, but also that the parents have lost a child. This is widely considered to be the most devastating loss across cultures. But the sudden loss of a parent can hit a child twice: they lose one of their parents and, at the same time, the other parent may be so affected that, for the child, it can be experienced as a double loss. In contrast, the loss of a grandparent may affect one parent more profoundly, but the other parent's ability to parent remains largely unaffected.

A death in the family will almost always mean that roles have to be reassigned, relationships can become difficult, and internal communication changes. The void left by the loss of a father or mother is difficult to fill, as is that left by the death of a sibling. Family members are often linked through different relationships and experiences throughout life, playing different roles in each other's lives. In addition to family missing the deceased in the activities that fill the relationships, death can also bring concerns about the death of others. And this worry can lead to changes such as overprotection of children by parents, strong fears about the absence of the surviving parent (separation anxiety), and mutual anxiety about the reactions seen in each other. Some children who used to be affectionate and seek physical contact may now be distant, while others have an increased need for closeness. Some parents impose rigid rules about indoor time and meals, while others let boundaries slip. Many families find that the atmosphere in the home is very different from before the death and that this lasts for a long time.

In this chapter, we relate ways to help not only the bereaved child but also the family to find a good way of coping and talking about the death at home. In addition, we give concrete advice on how parents can best support their grieving child and how professionals can work therapeutically with grieving families. Our aim is that after reading the chapter you will be better equipped to support and guide bereaved families, whatever your role.

Grief is a family affair: The importance of parental support

When a close family member dies, whether it's a child or a partner, parents are deeply impacted. If the death is sudden and traumatic, parents may also experience PTSD in addition to their grief. It's important to recognize that any support provided to parents is also essential support for their children. Grief can consume individuals, and if parents are struggling with intense emotions, their children will notice and be affected.

The support that parents receive from friends and family can compensate for the loss of parental involvement and presence that children may feel. Practical assistance can be particularly helpful, such as someone providing transportation to leisure activities, taking the children to the movies, or arranging play dates. Accepting such help demonstrates good parenting skills as it allows parents to process their grief while also providing necessary relief.

When a parent is bereaved, they may feel guilty about not being present enough for their children, even though it's natural to feel overwhelmed by grief. However, adults who accept their limitations and allow themselves to grieve will eventually become more present for their children. It's important for both parents and their support system to understand that there may be an imbalance in the give-and-take dynamic after such a loss, and the bereaved parent should not feel indebted to others.

After the death of a partner, the adult left behind must navigate the new role of being a single parent. They must take on practical tasks that were previously shared by two, and manage all the necessary paperwork and digital record keeping that goes with modern life. Above all, they must contend with the emotional void left behind, which includes a lack of someone to share their concerns and joys about their children's development and well-being.

As a parent coping with grief, it is important to seek help early if you are experiencing post-traumatic reactions beyond the first month, or if your grief becomes complicated (see Chapter 6). Prolonged grief, where the grief continues unabated month after month, can impair your ability to function at work and in the family, and is a common type of complicated grief in adults (Kristensen *et al.*, 2021).

Talking about what has changed in the family

When grief affects a family, it can be challenging to talk about, but it is essential to do so. Parents have a responsibility to put words to the feelings that arise and start a conversation with their children. Younger children's grief can be acknowledged by saying something about how they probably miss the deceased person being there when they need to eat, or when they need a lift to training or school. For the very youngest, death becomes understandable if it is explained to them, say, in this way: 'Now Daddy can never read to you again, and that's sad. You might feel sad or miss Daddy when you go to bed. But you can always have your dad in your heart, and you can think that he is with you and whispering good words in your ear.' With older children, you can explain a little more about why the deceased is particularly missed in certain situations, such as when the whole family is together at mealtimes, on holidays, or at celebrations.

When a child dies, it's important for siblings to understand that although their parents may be sad, things will eventually get better and that it is not their responsibility to comfort their parents. Adults may take longer to process grief than children, but it's normal for kids to be concerned about their parents and want to help. Parents should reassure their children that their grief will last a while, but time is a friend and things will improve. It's essential for parents to encourage their children to express their feelings and not feel as if they have to hide their grief to protect their parents. Additionally, parents can help their children understand that losing a sibling is just as hard as losing a child, and that they are loved and valued.

What can parents do for their children?

Throughout this book, we emphasize the significance of creating an open and supportive environment at home where death and the deceased can be discussed. During a prolonged period of illness or immediately following a sudden death, providing factual information is important.

Provide children with access to factual information

As adults, we have gained a wealth of experience over our lives, which allows us to understand the world around us, process complex situations, and identify resources to cope with them. However, children rely on adults to access and interpret what happened. Without adequate information, their understanding can be incomplete, leading to gaps that are filled by their imagination. Unfortunately, the short distance between imagination and anxiety means that without facts and support from adults, young children can quickly develop thoughts that it may be their fault that their parent has died, or develop fears about their own safety or the safety of their remaining parent.

Facts are therefore important for several reasons. It allows both children and adults to form a coherent picture of what has happened. By bringing together the events and arranging them along a timeline, this creates a framework that helps to reduce the burden of memory on the grieving family. Studies have shown that a complete picture is remembered better than an incomplete one, which is why 'hard facts', such as the method of death or the circumstances of the event, can help in understanding and even contribute positively to the healing process, despite the potential risk of trauma reactions.

In fact, the understanding and clarity that knowledge provides may offset the possible trauma impact. By providing children with the facts they need, parents and caregivers can help them make sense of the situation and avoid the confusion and anxiety that may arise from their imaginations. Thus, while the process may be challenging and painful, it is important to provide children with the facts they require to move forward in a healthy way.

When providing facts, it is important to be honest about the illness or death. Do your best to provide answers to the questions the child might have.

For illness:

- What illness does the parent have?

- What is the illness and what is known about it?

- What is going to happen now?

For death:

- How did the parent die?

- When did the parent die?

- What do we know [with unexpected deaths]?

- Do we know why it happened?

- Do we know who else has been informed?

Here, we offer some suggestions for what you can do to ensure that affected children are well informed.

Try to communicate various facts early on in a calm and confident way:

- Provide accurate information, without embellishment or unnecessary detail. For instance, in the case of a suicide, you can disclose that the person took their own life without describing graphic details. This way, you provide facts that are no more frightening than necessary.

- Encourage your child to ask questions, and anticipate that younger children may ask questions that differ from what you expect.

- Keep your child informed about any newknowledge that arises concerning the illness or death.

> The father of a boy who was approaching puberty had been killed. The boy drew a fantasy of his father being killed, expressing his grief and his longing to be reunited with his father. The mother shared some information she received from the police with her psychologist, including what they suspected happened during the killing, based on their investigation. One of the boy's drawings matched closely with the details that the police had identified. The psychologist urged the mother to share the facts with the boy, and she eventually did. After receiving factual information, the boy's tormenting fantasies were significantly reduced.

When adults don't share information with children, it's usually because they think the children are too young to understand their explanations, or because they're afraid the knowledge will hurt them too much. But if, by chance, a child later learns something that has been kept from them – for example, that it was a suicide and not a heart attack – it can create distrust between the child and the adults: 'What else haven't they told me?' Parents not infrequently find themselves in a dilemma and seek advice on how to convey facts that was initially kept hidden from children. Our clear professional advice is to be open from the start, so that secrets (or worse, 'family' secrets) don't take root. Also, make sure that the version told in the family is the same one that is communicated to school and others. Children quickly notice if different 'truths' are circulating, and this can create anxiety and distrust of adults.

Allow children to take part in situations where knowledge is passed on or 'facts' are experienced

Children can gain a deeper understanding of illness and death by being involved in various events such as: visiting the ill person in a hospital; seeing the deceased after a death; attending funerals, memorial services, and follow-up talks in hospitals; meeting emergency staff; and reviewing autopsy reports or medical records. These are typically situations that children are excluded from, but they can provide valuable insight into the temporal relationships and structure of what has been happening. When children are left out, they are deprived of the opportunity to more fully comprehend the situation and to piece together important information that can contribute to their overall understanding as they mature.

When a child experiences situations involving death or loss, they are often exposed to knowledge that can be difficult to process. This can lead to emotional pain in the moment and, in some cases, post-traumatic suffering that requires professional help. Balancing the potential trauma with the benefits of understanding what has been happening is important.

Somewhat surprisingly, research has shown that adult family members who are present when a close family member receives lifesaving first aid at home (e.g., CPR and use of a defibrillator) subsequently experience fewer post-traumatic stress reactions, anxiety, and depression than those who were not present (Jabre *et al.*, 2013).

The idea is that witnessing the events provides a better

understanding, which outweighs any potential traumatic effects. Additionally, studies (e.g., Omerov *et al.*, 2017) have shown that adults who discover a family member who has taken their own life do not experience more difficulties than those who were equally close to the deceased but did not find them. We believe that being present where important information is shared, or seeing the deceased, results in fewer distressing thoughts and helps balance the stress associated with the sensory impressions of being present. While these studies were conducted with adults, we believe the same applies to children. However, preparation and explanation are even more critical for children in these situations.

Information for understanding self or others

As a parent, you play an important role in helping your children understand and interpret their own and others' reactions during the grieving process. Children may experience shock, numbness, or intense emotions such as crying fits, which can make them feel scared or confused. Young people may wonder if they are going 'crazy' due to the intensity of their emotions.

It is important for calm and reassuring adults to help children and young people understand what is happening and why they are experiencing these reactions. Parents who have lost a child or spouse may find it challenging to support their children because they are experiencing their own strong emotions. However, providing children with a 'map' of the terrain they are moving into can be helpful, for example, explaining that it is common for children to think that they are to blame for what happened, but that it is not their fault.

If a child's reaction is not what they expected, parents can offer reassurance and explain that this is a normal response to the shock of the situation. For example, if a child does not feel as much sadness as they expected to, parents can explain that this may be due to the protective numbness of shock, but that as time goes on, they will likely experience more intense emotions. By providing context and reassurance, parents can help children navigate their grief and make sense of their emotions.

As a parent, you can also make other people's reactions more understandable.

> A teenage girl who had just lost her mother became furious with her cousin, who cried much more than she did during her mother's funeral. However, her anger subsided when someone explained to her that the shock she was feeling was actually a natural defence mechanism and that she needed it to protect her from the overwhelming pain of losing her mother. Her cousin, on the other hand, did not need that protection because she still had her mother. Understanding this helped the girl come to terms with her own emotions and realize that it was okay to feel the way she did.

Children may find it challenging to comprehend their friends' reactions after a loss. They may feel hurt and surprised when their friends seem to forget about their loss quickly. Parents can offer comfort by explaining that friends have their own lives and may not always remember the loss as the child does. It is essential for parents to increase the child's understanding of why this happens instead of apologizing for their friends' forgetfulness. This understanding may prevent children from withdrawing from friends who they feel do not understand their loss.

Children also need to understand why their parents react the way they do when dealing with grief. When parents are able to articulate their thoughts and emotions, it can ease children's concerns that their parents may not be able to take care of them, and minimize children's feelings that they need to 'walk on eggshells' around their parents. When parents explain their reactions, it can also dispel any misconceptions or unrealistic ideas children may have about how adults cope with grief, and prevent children from feeling overly responsible for their parents' well-being.

Providing psychoeducational information to children also helps them understand that grief is not experienced uniformly within a family and that family members may grieve differently and at different paces. For example, if a child in the family has passed away, one parent may be in a better emotional state than the other at the same time. Grief is variable, and this means that family members may experience it at different times and in different ways.

Other actions parents can take

When parents are not themselves directly affected by a loss, for example if a friend of their child dies, they may find that children and young people seek out other friends who are also grieving, or the family of the deceased, because they find more resonance for their grief there than at home. Parents must not let it become a competition to see who is the most supportive, but instead make it clear that they are there for the children and will answer questions as best they can and listen to what the children have to say.

Either way, it is important to let children and young people decide as much as possible when and how they want to talk about what has happened. If there are several siblings, the eldest may wait until the younger siblings have gone to bed. Although it can be exhausting because the adults need 'adult time', it is a good investment to go the extra mile to meet this young person's grief. Others choose to talk during a car ride because the conversation here – without direct eye contact – is less intense. If possible, follow the signals and initiatives of children and young people. After a death, they become sensitive to what they may experience as rejection, such as messages like 'I don't have time right now', or 'Can't it wait until tomorrow?'

Parents need to be mindful that their children are not assuming too much adult responsibility after a loss, such as attempting to take on the role of the deceased. Filling the void left by the person who has died, whether through practical tasks or through emotional support, can be overwhelming and exhausting for a child. While it is important for children to contribute to the household, by caring for younger siblings for example, parents must ensure that their children have the opportunity to be children and engage in age-appropriate activities with peers.

Research has demonstrated the importance of maintaining discipline in the family after a loss (Hagan *et al.*, 2011). This involves ensuring that the rules that were in place before the death continue to be upheld. It is understandable for parents to feel sympathetic towards their grieving child and allow certain rules to slip. However, it is essential to maintain stability and structure in the family by sticking to routines such as bedtime, indoor time, and household responsibilities. In this way, children can feel a sense of predictability and security during an otherwise chaotic and uncertain time.

According to research, creating a warm and accepting environment for children who have lost a parent can help them thrive in the years that follow (Hagan *et al.*, 2011). While there are few studies on the long-term effects of preventive interventions in families who have lost children, some studies have shown the positive impact of teaching parents effective strategies for interacting with their children (Sandler *et al.*, 2018) (see also Chapter 11, Therapy with Children).

After experiencing a painful loss, it can be challenging for parents to function as they did before. However, accepting offers of support and help, whether from friends or from professional assistance such as crisis teams, counsellors, or support associations, can aid in coping. Asking others for help may be difficult, but it's important to remember that others are often willing to help. Seeking outside support or asking for help is necessary to be able to help your children.

'It won't be the same as before. Your capacity is not as great as when there were two. I think that's an important lesson, especially regarding the role of a mother. What does it look like when

a puzzle with four pieces now only has three pieces left? That process can be challenging. It also means that you may need to improve your ability to accept help. If you're someone who prefers to do things independently, that can actually be quite difficult.'
Bereaved mother

Therapeutic work with grief in families

Our recommendation is for early involvement of professionals who can provide ongoing support to families following the death of a child or parent. This does not have to be an extensive follow-up, but rather three to five sessions during the first year after the death, preferably with professionals who specialize in bereavement and family dynamics. We have described such a follow-up in an article (Pereira *et al.*, 2017), which is further discussed in Chapter 11, Therapy with Children. Professionals working with children who have lost a close family member also emphasize the necessity of early intervention (A. Dyregrov *et al.*, 2020a).

The main purpose of these follow-up sessions is to help the family communicate about what has happened and how the individual is feeling, as well as to provide advice on, for example, children's participation in rituals, interaction with the environment, and good coping skills. At the same time, parents who have received such early support say it is an effective way to get started. The conversations provide space to make a plan for moving forward, talk about the things that worry the family, and build an understanding of what needs to happen next.

The family sessions are tailored to address the specific needs that arise during the initial conversation with the parent(s) and child. It is possible that important information has not been shared within the family, which may hinder a complete understanding of the events. This is particularly important for children who may have been shielded from such information and need a fuller understanding of the circumstances. This can involve reviewing accident reports with the police or autopsy reports with a doctor. Additionally, it may be beneficial for both parents and children to meet with emergency personnel or visit the hospital where their loved one died. In some cases, visiting the scene of the incident together and engaging in a shared ritual can help mark the end of a period of grief.

Conclusion

The death of a loved one can be an overwhelming experience that weighs heavily on the entire family. It's common for parents to feel critical of their ability to support their children during this challenging time. It's important to remember that no one is expected to have the same energy and resources when dealing with grief and loss. Accepting help and support from others, reflecting on the new role and situation, and talking openly and honestly with children about the changes they're experiencing can create a solid foundation for the family's future.

While it can be challenging, setting up a framework where both the difficult and good days and memories can be shared makes it easier to get through the loss together as a family. By communicating openly about facts, thoughts, and feelings and recognizing that it takes time to adjust to life without the deceased, the family can become stronger and more connected than ever before. Remember, this experience is something that can bring family members closer together and strengthen the family, rather than creating distance.

Chapter 9

Grief and Relationships: Navigating Loss with Children and Adolescents

Introduction: Children's relationships during illness and bereavement

This chapter provides tools and knowledge to support children dealing with grief, as well as an understanding of how different losses affect their situation and how to define your role and boundaries. By the end of the chapter, readers will gain insight into how to help bereaved children with their relationships at home and among friends, as well as a comprehensive understanding of the areas affected by loss and the support needs that arise as a consequence.

Children's lives can be abruptly transformed when they experience life-threatening illness or grief, particularly if they come from a predictable and secure background. Suddenly, a family member may be in hospital or missing altogether, disrupting their otherwise familiar daily lives. Research (Dowdney, 2000; Green & Connolly, 2009) has shown that such situations can be very stressful for children, who may lack experience in dealing with life crises. Younger children, in particular, may not have the necessary development to fully comprehend the situation (Hunter & Smith, 2008).

However, in the face of illness and grief, it is important to recognize that children are not an isolated entity. Numerous researchers (e.g., Burns *et al.*, 2015; Ennis & Majid, 2021; Götze *et al.*, 2018; Holmgren, 2021) have documented how parents often struggle with their own grief and lack of energy in the time following the loss of a close family member. This can create an unfortunate situation where parents do not have the capacity to help children cope with the difficult emotions they are experiencing. Additionally, many parents often feel they lack the knowledge and tools to provide the necessary support. This is problematic because studies (e.g., Høeg *et al.*, 2018, 2019) have shown that children who do not receive help from adults after a death have worse outcomes in life than children from non-bereaved families.

Just as families can be overwhelmed by the difficult emotions that accompany illness and loss, it can be difficult for friends to know how to talk about the situation and what support they can provide. Studies (Lytje, 2016b; Winther-Lindqvist & Olund Larsen, 2021) have described how both friends and classmates find the task of being a support person difficult. Many bereaved children report finding that some friends withdraw as a result – not necessarily out of ill will, but because they do not know how to support or be with the affected friend. This can be particularly challenging for young people who, in addition to struggling with a difficult family situation, may also feel different or experience isolation or bullying.

It's important to recognize that grief can follow children into all aspects of their lives, including their family, nursery, school, extracurricular activities, and informal friendship groups. As a result, it's essential to make these arenas supportive and understanding places for the child rather than places that reinforce a sense of isolation and difference. This requires not only supporting the family's work with grief but also providing friends with the knowledge and tools to support the affected child.

How illness and grief can affect children's connections with others

In order to provide effective support for children's relationships during times of illness and after death, it is important to understand the various reasons why these relationships may become uncertain and impacted during these difficult times. It is important to note that each situation is unique, and different trajectories can present their own set of challenges.

Both personal emotional challenges and practical circumstances can take a toll on relationships. In terms of emotions, children may experience anxiety and/or sadness for an extended period of time. Life-threatening illnesses may lead to fear and uncertainty, while grief can result in feelings of confusion, excessive thoughts, anxiousness, and a lack of energy. Children experiencing a crisis may also have trouble sleeping, which can further exacerbate these issues. All of these factors can make it difficult for children to maintain normal levels of energy and patience, and may even lead to irritability and anger.

It's important to understand that children often feel that their situation is unique and difficult for others to understand if they have not experienced something similar. Comparing the loss of a grandparent or pet to the loss of a sibling or parent is rarely well received, even if friends are trying to offer support. Such comparisons may be perceived as insulting, and a lack of empathy and understanding can lead to awkward situations if children and their friends are not provided with a framework for discussing what has happened.

Bereavement due to deaths, such as suicide or murder, can further complicate relationships for the grieving individual. Such deaths are often difficult to talk about, and some may choose to conceal them or tell a different story. However, this can cause confusion for children affected by the death, who may not know if they are allowed to discuss the event, and may ultimately withdraw from friendships. Although it can be challenging to face the truth in the short term, concealing the cause of death can lead to alternative explanations and secrets becoming a greater burden over time.

In addition to emotional challenges, practical tasks that need to be taken on at home can also interfere with a child's ability to maintain friendships. Older children, in particular, may assume practical responsibilities during a family illness or after a death, when an adult is suddenly absent from the household. Such responsibilities can include cooking, cleaning, shopping, and caring for younger siblings. The eldest child is particularly at risk here, as they may have the best foundation for taking on these roles. While children may be willing to help family members, it can come at the cost of their own time and ability to see friends. It may be necessary for adults to help find a balance between supporting the family and allowing the child to socialize, as otherwise the child may become socially isolated in the long term.

Working with children's relationships

In this section, we explore how you, as a support worker, can assist children in preserving their relationships during life-threatening illnesses and after a loss. This includes offering guidance for managing relationships within the home as well as among peers and friends.

As described previously, life-threatening illness doesn't just impact children; it can have far-reaching effects on the entire family. Studies have shown that parents, in particular, can find it challenging to balance the day-to-day demands of caring for an ill child while also maintaining some sense of normalcy in their lives. In cases where a parent dies, the family can suddenly face a significant absence of emotional support and practical assistance from an adult figure.

Although welfare systems and insurance options are available in many western countries, economic threats can still arise. Such challenges are often most significant for families with low income, unemployment, or where the deceased was self-employed.

When families experience crises, multiple factors come into play. The adults in the family need to possess the necessary knowledge and resilience to support their children through difficult times and establish appropriate frameworks for dealing with the situation internally. Ultimately, factors such as the parents' own grief, available social resources, and financial stability can all impact the situation at home.

Research indicates that parents often require support in helping their children cope with loss and are willing to work with nurseries and schools to create a supportive environment for their children (Lytje & Dyregrov, 2021). While parents are the primary source of support for children, grief can have a profound impact on parents, and they may themselves require additional referral to support services.

Both professionals and the family's social network can openly inquire about how the family is coping and listen to what the children know about what has happened – as well as ask about their thoughts on death and life after death. If a child's frame of reference is that their parent is in heaven, it is important that this is also the starting point in discussions with support people. It is important to seek additional help if there are problems in the home that may affect the child's well-being or their relationships with the remaining family members. Warning signs may include not talking about what is happening in the home, or the child spending all their time away from the family. A conversation with parents or the surviving parent may also be a good opportunity to ask if they are getting the help they need, or if support needs should be passed on to a patient organization or health system.

The golden rule is that the earlier a family gets help, the sooner they can address the things that are not working. If parents ask for advice on how to deal with their new life situation, research shows that open communication is hugely important (Saldinger *et al.*, 2004). Children want to be included and mourn together with their family. If they are not allowed to do so, they often end up dealing with their grief alone, which can lead to resentment towards their family (Lytje & Dyregrov, 2021). Other research also shows that children whose parents are open and supportive after a death cope better both in the immediate aftermath and throughout their lives (Luecken *et al.*, 2009; Worden, 1996).

If a family lives with a life-threatening illness, it's not certain that you will experience much concern during your first conversation with them. However, it's important to remember that things can quickly change, and the family can be further burdened if the illness worsens or is prolonged. New challenges may arise in the family that need to be addressed, and as a support person, you can help alleviate them.

Therefore, it's a good idea to ensure that there is a good plan for future communication with the family, both when you're worried and when you're not. As a teacher or healthcare professional, this can be in the form of scheduled meetings or through other forms of contact, such as regular updates on an intranet. Especially in situations where you're concerned, we recommend physical meetings. These meetings often provide a better sense of what's going on and give parents more time to ask questions or talk about their daily lives. Although such meetings can be difficult, as they deal with 'heavy topics', we've found that parents appreciate them. They also provide parents with a space to open up and talk about their concerns. However, it's always a good idea to have two professionals present at such a meeting, if resources permit. This way, you're not alone with your thoughts leading up to the meeting, and you have someone to share the responsibility of the conversation with.

If you, as a support person, notice that the family is having difficulty talking about the illness or death and you consider that this is weakening family dynamics, it's important to address the issues you see. Is it because the parents don't know how to talk about what happened? Do the parents have misconceptions, such as thinking that mentioning the deceased will upset the children? In these cases, it's often enough to provide some specific perspectives and guidance on why it's important to be able to remember the deceased together. Here, pamphlets and other written information from relevant websites can be helpful.

If you notice mental health problems in a parent, such as depression, it's a good idea to refer them for psychological help. And if you wish, you can offer to facilitate the contact, ensuring that the parent gets this help. If there's a lack of structural resources, such as aid with practical things at home or transportation to extracurricular activities, it's a good idea to see if parents in the child's class or the family's social network can support and relieve the affected parent.

Working with the child's relationships involves being attentive to the child's well-being and being open to considering and discussing issues as they arise. Children are constantly developing, gaining new understandings of themselves and their families. This can lead to strengthened relationships but also new problems, making it important to have a conversation partner who can provide new perspectives and help when needed. Child professionals are ideally positioned to take on that role.

We will now look at two types of loss that can particularly impact families: the loss of a parent and the loss of a sibling. Parents or surviving parents have the most important role in supporting and taking care of their children. In the following sections, we describe important aspects of parents' relationships with each other and the help that parents can provide.

Supporting children after the loss of a partner: The role of the remaining parent

Losing a parent is many children's greatest fear in childhood, and it is without doubt the most profound loss a child can experience. Not only do they lose one parent, but they may also find that the other parent is so affected by the loss that it feels like partly having lost the other parent too. In Chapter 8, Grief in the Family, we described how the loss of a partner can weaken parenting capacity.

Children perceive this as early as pre-school age, and they want to comfort and be there for the parent: 'Don't be sad, Mum, you have me.' Children may feel greater responsibility or may grow to accept responsibility by helping more at home, but often they will also push their own thoughts and reactions away so that the remaining parent does not have to worry further or suffer more than he or she already does.

To support the children, the surviving parent should aim to create a stable and loving home environment with consistent rules for indoor time, bedtime, and household responsibilities. While grieving is a natural process, the parent can try to normalize the situation at home. Accepting practical help from others can help with managing the overwhelming loss. Enlist others to assist with tasks such as cooking or taking the children to activities, and consider having a trusted friend or family member organize the support to ensure it can be sustained over time.

As a parent, it is essential to receive support early on, particularly if the death has resulted in intrusive memories or thoughts that are troubling you. If left unaddressed, these issues can weaken your parenting capacity after the first few weeks. Seeking help with these specific problems can also benefit your children, as it enables you to be more present for them. It can be challenging to talk to children about the deceased if every conversation brings back memories of how your partner died. While it is important not to push grief away, it is advisable to seek help with any traumatic aspects of the death so that the grief becomes more manageable.

Grief can be an overwhelming experience, and it's essential to take breaks from it. Finding a balance between approaching the loss to process it and taking breaks to resume daily functions can be difficult. While it's normal for grief to be almost ever-present early after a loss, over time it's important to be able to gain distance from the pain and gradually resume a more normal life. This is especially important for maintaining a sense of normality in the home and supporting the well-being of your children.

As a parent, you can explain to your children that adults often feel sadder than children do when they experience grief. Children have many things that take their minds off the loss, but adults live with the loss all the time. You can reassure your children that it's okay to see you cry and that they are not responsible for making you happy again. It's a sad time, and adults feel it more than children, but it gets better with time.

Invite your children to talk, but don't force them. They may want to talk in the car or in the evening before bed when they feel the loss more acutely. Seize the opportunity when they take the initiative to talk. Ask open-ended questions such as, 'Are you wondering where Dad is now?' If so, 'What are you thinking?' or, 'What thoughts come up when you are at school?' Questions that can't be answered with a simple 'yes' or 'no' make for better conversations that help develop children's understanding and give space for the emotions they are experiencing. When you put into words some of your thoughts and feelings and how you cope with longing, you serve as a good role model for your children, helping them learn to regulate their emotions.

Turning up the volume on emotions may not sound pleasant, but many young people regulate their emotions to the point where they turn them down or hide them altogether. This is described in Chapter 6, Complicated Grief Processes. They may also fear opening up about their feelings because they fear being overwhelmed. Gently telling your children how to approach their grief and talking about what it means to have a parent who has died can help them learn that it doesn't mean falling into a deep hole. It's important not to push children and young people who keep their feelings at a distance too hard, as they may shut down completely. Short conversations with them can be helpful, and be sure to accept it if they quickly close them.

As mentioned earlier, traumatic circumstances can create problems for parents' grief, but also for children, as the following example shows.

> Two siblings witnessed their father collapsing at home due to heart problems, which led to ambulance staff arriving and administering lifesaving first aid. While their father received treatment in the living room, the children were asked to wait in the hallway. Despite attempts to revive him using a defibrillator, their father ultimately passed away. Unfortunately, the children saw everything through a window in the door and have been haunted by the intrusive memory of their father's body 'jumping up' as a result of the electric shocks from the defibrillator. It was crucial that these two siblings received help to process this traumatic experience.

This kind of experience brings back painful memories, and surviving parents or other adults should be alert if children are struggling with this kind of specific problem, so they can get early help.

When a parent dies, it creates a significant void in the family dynamic. The tasks and responsibilities that the deceased parent once carried out must be taken over by others. These may include practical tasks around the home as well as emotional and supportive functions that the deceased fulfilled. It can be challenging for families to discuss how to redistribute these roles, but it's important to do so. Sometimes, surviving parents may try to take on the role of the other parent in supporting and encouraging the children, only to be met with resistance. It can be helpful to seek the guidance of a professional with experience in familial conversations to facilitate discussions about how the family was before the death and how it will be going forward.

As a surviving parent, it's important to acknowledge that you cannot take on all the responsibilities of your deceased partner. It's also important to recognize if your child is trying to take on too many tasks that you are not able to handle. Children can become what's known as 'parentified', where they assume adult responsibilities that weigh down their childhood. While it's natural for children to take on more practical responsibilities after a death due to the reduction in the number of people in the household, taking on the role of a 'back-up parent' for younger siblings can quickly become overwhelming. It's challenging to define where the line should be drawn, but it's important that children do not assume adult responsibilities that are too weighty.

> After the sudden death of their father, the family's 14-year-old daughter took charge. She took on the responsibility of calling the appropriate authorities, contacting the funeral director and insurance company, and caring for her 10-year-old brother when their mother broke down. Despite the mother recovering slightly after a few days, the daughter continued to take the lead. It was only after discussing the changes in roles after the death that the pattern gradually shifted and the mother could begin to regain control.

As a surviving parent, it can be challenging to create a warm and comforting environment for your children after the loss of their other parent. Shared meals may be particularly difficult, with an empty seat at the table. However, mealtimes are an essential aspect of family life, and it is best to maintain this focal point for your 'new' family. Talk to your children about how difficult it is not to be able to sit together as a whole family, but emphasize the importance of continuing to gather for meals. To make it a pleasant experience again, you must make a concerted effort and push yourselves, even if it is painful in the beginning. Consider moving the table or sitting at a different spot, but always prioritize the shared meals.

Parental help for children after the loss of a sibling

The loss of a child is a devastating experience, not only for parents but also for the siblings left behind. Many of the resources available for supporting families after the death of a parent can also be helpful in this situation. However, while there are often two parents who can provide care and support for the remaining children, the loss of a child generally causes pain unlike any other loss, and both parents may struggle to cope. This is where support from the wider community can be essential. While both parents may be affected, it is rare for them to be equally affected at the same time.

When a child is ill, it's important to acknowledge that the relationships between siblings can be affected by negative thoughts and feelings. Even if siblings have a strong bond, the healthy child may feel left out and neglected as all the parental attention is focused on the ill child. This can lead to feelings of jealousy and even thoughts that it would be better if the ill sibling were no longer there, which may result in guilt after that child's death. Parents can alleviate this guilt by acknowledging and discussing these potential feelings with their children. Additionally, adults who are aware of this situation, such as teachers, can show extra attention and explain to the healthy child why the parents are spending more time with the ill sibling. In conversations with parents, they can be encouraged to prioritize the healthy child whenever possible.

Children who witness parental grief may struggle with feelings of guilt and comparisons between themselves and their deceased siblings. They may think that their parents would have grieved less if they had died instead, or feel inadequate in comparison to their sibling. It's important for parents to communicate that they would grieve equally for any of their children, and to normalize the range of emotions they are experiencing. However, navigating grief is hard for parents, and they may require support and resources to address their own grief and help their children cope.

In some instances, children may be present during their sibling's death or learn about it through the death notification. They may also survive accidents in which a sibling dies. In these situations, parents may be preoccupied with the events surrounding the death, leaving little attention for the surviving siblings. It's important for parents and other adults to be aware of potential trauma effects on them; they may experience strong sensory impressions and require additional support.

After the death of a sibling, parents may become overprotective of their surviving children, which can increase anxiety and make the situation more difficult for them. It's helpful for children if parents address their children's anxiety and gradually help them develop independence. This can involve letting them go out unsupervised and communicating clearly about schedules and plans. Friends and neighbours can also play a role by encouraging children to keep their parents informed of their whereabouts.

The absence of a child can be strongly felt if the remaining siblings attend the same school and see classmates of the brother or sister they have lost. When bereaved siblings have to navigate through a landscape of memories, the absence of someone they went to school with or the realization that it is no longer possible to do what they did together in the afternoons or during holidays can trigger yearning and longing. When bereaved children were asked to describe what they missed most about their sibling after the killings at Utøya in Norway on 22 July, 2011, one boy wrote 'someone to fight with'.

It's important to keep in mind that during a hospitalization for illness, the ill child's friends may ask the healthy sibling many questions, which can be stressful. Teachers who are attentive can serve as sounding boards if the siblings find this uncomfortable.

Providing words of support that acknowledge the difficulty of the situation and offer hope that things will improve over time can also be helpful. However, it's also important to encourage the remaining siblings to confront the absence of their lost brother or sister rather than avoid it. We delve deeper into this topic in Chapter 6, Complicated Grief Processes.

Working with children's relationships among friends

Ensuring positive relationships among bereaved children's friends involves both providing support for the friends they have chosen and creating a supportive environment in the child's social settings, such as their school class or nursery group.

Studies show that many children find it difficult to return to the institution, and challenging to be met by peers who have no experience of dealing with their new life situation (Jørgensen *et al.*, 2019; Lytje, 2016a; Asgari & Naghavi, 2020). Here, an initial lack of guidance can quickly lead to the child concerned feeling different and isolated, which can lead to mistrust and bullying. Interestingly, a Danish study shows that bereaved children are both bullied and also bully themselves more than children who have not lost a loved one (Nielsen *et al.*, 2012). To prevent such problems, it is essential that bereaved children are met with understanding and compassion from their peers and friends. As an adult, you can help by using your knowledge and experience to prepare friends and peers for interactions with the bereaved child. Additionally, it is important to remember that the child may have friends in other classes and age groups who may also require guidance.

Anticipating any potential changes in life circumstances related to a life-threatening illness is constructive planning. Start by considering the individual needs and experiences of the child, including how much involvement they desire from their class and whether they require support in informing their friends. If you are a staff member, it's essential to help create a supportive framework for the child's successful return. If you have another role, it's beneficial to reach out to the school or nursery to understand how they approach these issues and raise awareness of the need for support.

Keep in mind that the child's situation and support needs may evolve over time, particularly in the case of illness. It's essential to establish a way to receive continuous updates on the ill person's progress and relapses so that you can be prepared to offer support during difficult times and avoid missing changing needs. It's important to remember that a life-threatening illness can be as demanding as death itself, and children may require guidance and support early in the process to navigate friendships while coping with difficult emotions.

It is important to be aware that in some cases, particularly in grief, children may not want anyone to know about their situation or may be very selective about who is informed. Such reactions are often a way for children to control what they can in the midst of chaos and to avoid feeling as if they are losing control over their lives. However, it is important to involve friends in what is going on and to avoid letting the child pick and choose who is informed. If some friends know more than others, it can lead to rumours and hurt feelings. It is best if everyone has the same information or a common 'story', which is why it is important for the family, the child's institution, and anyone else involved to all communicate the same facts.

If the child is reluctant to have information shared, it is important to explain why it is helpful to do so. However, ultimately, following a sudden death, classmates and friends have the right to know what has happened, as uncertainty can create a breeding ground for broken relationships. Therefore, it may be necessary to share facts, even if the child does not want to. If classmates and friends do not know what is going on, they cannot provide proper support.

It can be helpful if teachers initiate separate conversation with the child's friends from different schools to discuss how to handle loss and offer support. With the child's close friends, teachers can go deeper and create specific rules and support systems that may not be necessary for the whole class. This type of support can be particularly helpful for younger children, but it is relevant for older students as well. It is good to check with the child to see if this is something they would like. Here is some advice that can be given to friends:

- Reach out to those affected early on; don't avoid contact.

- A simple gesture such as a letter, a flower, or a small greeting can bring comfort.

- A hug can also provide warmth and comfort, if appropriate.

- Show that you care and are willing to help in any way possible.

- Avoid reaching out just out of curiosity – be sincere in your intentions.

- Don't assume you understand how your friend feels – listen and validate their emotions.

- Be cautious about giving unsolicited advice on how to react or handle the situation.

- Ask your friend if they want to talk about what has happened or just spend time together as normal.

- Allow space for grief, but also remember that your friend is still the same person as before and may still enjoy normal activities.

- Respect that everyone grieves differently and be patient with those who struggle for a long time.

- Encourage participation in social activities, sports, get-togethers, and walks as a way to promote social connections and self-care.

This advice is primarily aimed at older children, but can be adapted for younger children in a developmentally appropriate way. For more information on how to approach grief in children of different ages, please refer to Chapter 3, Development and Children's Grief.

Support following the loss of a close friend

Some of our research has focused on the impact of losing close friends, and we conducted a study in 1999 (A. Dyregrov *et al.*, 1999a, 1999b) which demonstrated the significant effects experienced by friends and classmates following the loss of a friend. Further research has confirmed that the degree of closeness to the deceased person is directly related to the intensity and duration of grief or trauma reactions (Poijula *et al.*, 2001; Servaty-Seib & Pistole, 2007).

Again, parents will be central in helping their children. However, there is a significant difference in that parents themselves are less directly affected by the loss. This means that they can be more present and helpful in their children's grief, as they struggle less with their own reactions. At the same time, children and young people can turn to the parents of the deceased because they feel that their grief is similar to their own, and therefore they under-stand the young people's situation better than their own parents do. Parents must of course accept this, while knowing that it is up to the bereaved parents themselves to decide how ready they feel to be visited by their child's friends. At first, this is both good and bad for most parents – good to have friends thinking of them, but at the same time hard to see them because they remind them so much of the loss they have suffered. Over time, needs will change. Bereaved parents may want to maintain contact with the friends of the deceased, while friends become preoccupied with recreat-ing their lives without feeling that they need to be there for the bereaved parents.

Good adult support is important in helping friends cope with the loss of a friend. This support includes ensuring that friends are well informed after the death, creating opportunities for people to get together and support each other, and marking the event together. Talking together about what has happened can be par-ticularly helpful early on after the death, to provide an overview and context for the event and to mobilize joint support. Over time, what can be most important for friends is togetherness with others and the understanding that their deceased friend is still in their thoughts.

The impact of the loss of a friend can be easily overlooked, and grief over their death is not yet fully recognized. Children and young people may feel alone with their thoughts and may experi-ence feelings of guilt and shame, such as not spending enough time with their friend during an illness or not realizing that their friend was struggling with suicidal thoughts. Therefore, it is important for adults to pay attention, ask about their well-being over time, and acknowledge the significance of the loss. Otherwise, most of what has already been written about grief after the loss of a parent or sibling applies here as well.

New relationships

While it is essential for a child to have supportive friendships and family relationships, there may be needs that cannot be met through these existing connections, such as the opportunity to mirror their own grief experience in that of other peers. In such cases, initiatives like grief groups can provide a valuable opportunity for the child to see how others are feeling and recognize that they are not alone in their grief. These groups provide a safe and regular space for children to talk about difficult thoughts and ask questions without fear of upsetting friends or family members.

Participating in a grief group may not replace regular friendships, but it can provide a haven of comfort and support for children during days when their loss may feel quite overwhelming. Unfortunately, the availability of bereavement groups may vary depending on the location and the resources in the community.

It's common and quite understandable for children to feel nervous about attending a bereavement group for the first time. To help ease any anxiety, it may be beneficial to give the group a try once or twice and then assess whether it's the right thing for the child. However, if the child is completely resistant, it's okay to put the offer aside for the time being. You can always consider bringing it up again later when they are further along in the grieving process.

Recognize that everyone grieves differently, and while some children may need support right away, for others it may take years to be ready to seek help.

For older children, in particular, it can be valuable to receive support and perspective from peers, rather than just from adults. If a bereavement group isn't available in your area, consider enabling the child to have conversations with either a psychologist or some other adult in a position to help, to provide a similar space to vent concerns and gain support. The key is to find a safe and supportive environment for the child to express their feelings, no matter the form that support takes.

Your role in working with children's relationships

In working with children's relationships, questions can easily arise such as what your role is as a carer and how far you can afford to go in your work to support children and their families. The level of involvement may vary depending on your relationship with the child and their family, as well as your professional role. As a starting point, however, our advice is that you should be prepared to do more than you are comfortable with. Sometimes it's about daring to call the difficult meeting or ask some honest questions, even when the answers may be uncomfortable, because while these kinds of conversations can feel 'heavy' and stressful, they're also necessary to give you the knowledge you need to best support a grieving child.

If you are a professional who works with children, it's important to remember that you're not the only source of support for the child and their family. If you become the primary support person for multiple children and their families, you risk becoming overwhelmed and burning out. To avoid this, it's important to set boundaries and be mindful of your energy levels. If you want to provide sustained support over time, you need to manage your energy carefully.

As a teacher, educator, friend, or family member, your role is to support the grieving child. However, it's important to recognize that good help for the child often involves supporting the adults in the family as well. It can be emotionally and physically taxing to be there for both the child and the adults, so it's essential to ensure that you have the resources and stamina to provide ongoing support.

This may mean referring the family to support services specific to their situation or providing useful information on how to start their own bereavement work. You can also offer to make phone calls on their behalf, with their approval. Supporting the adults in the family can ultimately benefit the child in their grief journey.

Conclusion

It's important to remember that a few well-timed words of advice from other adults to concerned parents can make a huge difference in ensuring that families get off to a good start, rather than being broken down and fragmented by difficult situations. While parents provide the most important support for their children, it is often essential that they have access to social networks and various professional helpers, from educators to therapists, who can provide ongoing support. To ensure that children's lives are kept as intact as possible, it's important that these different systems work together and complement each other. When parents feel that they are working with professionals in their children's lives to get through a difficult time, such support is often judged as being the most effective. Cooperation gives both parents and children reassurance in a difficult situation, and it's best to ensure that children can continue to thrive despite the challenges they face.

Chapter 10

Navigating Grief in the Classroom: A Guide for Schools

Introduction: Why should the school play a role?

> 'My children spend six to eight hours a day at school, and I believe it's essential for them to have adults there who understand their individual stories, who know them for who they are, and who are aware of their struggles.' *Torben, surviving father of two school-aged children*

Next to the child's parents, the class teachers and members of the school's educational team are the adults who often spend the most time with the child during the week. They have a unique opportunity to make a significant difference in supporting children who are grieving. Their special insight into the personality, character, and individual needs of bereaved children enables them to offer tailored support. This familiarity and presence in the children's lives also create a special motivation to help children in crisis rediscover their joy of life and well-being. As a consequence, schools and nurseries have a central role to play in supporting children through grief and loss.

However, as professionals, we often face confusion about the role that schools and their personnel should play when a pupil is in the midst of a crisis. Teachers may feel uncertain about the boundary between their caring role and their obligation to fulfil educational tasks. This challenge is compounded by the fact that grieving pupils often have mixed feelings about the support they need. While they desire to be seen and understood, at the same time they may not want too much attention. This ambiguity often arises due to uncertainty about their new life situation, rather than a desire to be left alone. Several studies with both parents and children highlight the importance of schools supporting bereaved children by proactively helping them navigate their changed circumstances (Jørgensen *et al.*, 2019; Lytje, 2017). Furthermore, it has been found that effective support and a positive school re-entry experience can help reduce negative consequences in both the short and long term.

This chapter focuses on how schools and their personnel can optimize their efforts to support teachers, parents, and pupils during difficult times such as the loss of a loved one. We examine various factors that can impact all types of losses, and provide specific points of attention for life-threatening illnesses and sudden forms of death. This chapter is particularly relevant for those working in primary and secondary schools, with the goal of helping them establish a strong support system for children who have experienced the death of a close family member. Our aim is to guide schools in identifying the areas that require particular attention during this process and to provide you with basic knowledge of how the pupil's life is affected and where there may be a need for extra support.

School-related challenges in connection to life-threatening illness and death

When a pupil experiences a life-threatening illness or death in their immediate family, many aspects of life are difficult. Although school in that situation may seem like a safe haven, many of the difficulties follow them into this arena.

Research has found that grieving pupils may experience a decline in academic performance in the period leading up to and following a loss (see Chapter 4, The Impact of Loss on Children's Lives). This can lead to poorer grades and impair the child's chances of progressing in the education system. In addition, challenges may arise that hinder the child's personal and academic well-being. Reduced motivation is often a factor, especially if the deceased parent was responsible for motivating the child and supporting homework. During a time when the home is marked by grief, the surviving parent may not always have the resources to take on this role. The child might experience a sense of meaninglessness and view the loss as an example of how life is unpredictable, leading them to feel that it doesn't make sense to devote energy to schoolwork.

Intrusive memories and fantasies can also present significant issues that disrupt a child's concentration and memory. Memories may suddenly come to the forefront, such as images of when the child saw their deceased parent, or scenes from the funeral. The fantasies may relate to the child's perceived responsibility for (or inability to prevent) the parent's death, leading to feelings of guilt. These thoughts and memories can be very disturbing, affect the child's well-being, and detract from their schoolwork. Many parents report that grief and intrusive memories often arise at bedtime, which can lead to a negative spiral where the child does not get enough sleep, further weakening their concentration.

Grieving children commonly withdraw socially in the period leading up to and after a death. They often lack experience in how to discuss difficult experiences with others and may fear being perceived as different or making their friends uncomfortable by mentioning the loss. This difficulty is particularly pronounced for older children. The inability to share their struggles with friends can lead to a grieving pupil isolating themselves and feeling alone. This can further weaken their ability to perform academically. If the child's social relationships at school are not supportive, or if they are subjected to bullying, they may feel that academic success is unimportant.

Changes in the home can also affect the child's well-being before and after a loss, especially when the remaining family members themselves struggle with individual grief reactions, and their ability to care for the child may be diminished. This is particularly evident in cases of violent and unexpected deaths, where parents struggle with strong grief and post-traumatic reactions. In such situations, you may sometimes find that the parent(s) and the child have opposing needs. For example, the parents may not want to tell the child what has happened, but the child knows that something is being kept secret.

There are thus many difficulties that can affect the child's everyday life when a crisis strikes their family. In such a situation, school can become a refuge for the child if it can proactively accommodate their needs. Apart from these general risk factors, specific aspects of the child's life can also impact the support they require. These factors will be examined in greater detail in the next section.

Exploring the factors that shape grief and support needs

While every bereaved child's experience is unique, there are certain universal factors that directly affect the form and effectiveness of support initiatives. These factors include the child's age, the socio-economic resources available to the family, and the circumstances surrounding the death. By understanding these factors, it becomes possible to tailor support measures that address the specific needs of grieving children and provide them with effective care.

Age
The age of a grieving pupil is an important factor in determining the appropriate support. With younger children, teachers often

play a more significant role in providing assistance than peers. However, grief processes at this age may be less complex, as the difficulty of addressing death is not yet as prevalent. Friends may naturally ask questions and express curiosity about the loss, and young children may explore the concept of death through play. While adults may find it uncomfortable to see children playing burial in a sandbox, it is essential to avoid imposing our fears and reactions on them. For children, play is a natural way to make sense of death, and abruptly interrupting it may be more upsetting than the play itself.

While some researchers have claimed that it is not until the age of nine that children have the same understanding of death as an adult, in practice this can vary depending on the child's individual maturity and previous experience with death. However, it's important to be mindful of your language use and choose words that are clear and straightforward. For example, saying, 'Dad has died' is easier to understand than saying 'Dad has passed away', which could be interpreted in different ways. Using vague or abstract language can create confusion or even fear, as children may wonder if their loved one is in a place they know or if they can still visit them.

Note that for older children, especially teenagers, support from friends is generally considered more important than that received from adults. However, many teenagers feel that it is difficult to fit in and be 'normal' when dealing with a life-threatening illness or the loss of a close family member. Therefore, it is important to ensure not only that support is coming from you, but also that classmates and friends have the necessary tools to provide support. Friends may not have experience in supporting a grieving peer, and therefore they too need guidance and resources. In such cases, an important part of your role may be to set up some guidelines for how to talk about what has happened in a way that is comfortable for everyone involved.

Socio-economic resources

When families experience a life-threatening illness or the death of a loved one, they undergo significant changes that can have a ripple effect on the child's life. In the case of a parent's death, there may be financial strains that make it difficult for the family to maintain their current living situation or afford the child's extracurricular activities. While some families have life insurance which helps alleviate some of these issues, such insurance might not be purchased by vulnerable families who may already be struggling. As a result, children from such families can be disproportionately affected, and their access to leisure activities may be restricted or they may have to change schools.

As a teacher, friend, or family member, it's important to consider how you can support the child and family during this time of transition. One way to support the child is by exploring options to alleviate financial burdens that could impact their education and spare time activities, such as offering a school bursary or reduced sports club fees. Also, local government agencies in some countries may offer financial assistance. If the child must change schools due to the loss, it is essential to ensure that the new school is equipped to provide the necessary support and resources to help the child navigate their grief. Remember that any changes can be difficult for children, but they can be especially hard for those who are already facing additional stressors in their lives.

Although a child's loss of a family member can bring about significant changes, it's important to recognize that some things may stay the same. For instance, pre-existing family issues may persist or even intensify in the wake of the loss. Therefore, it's important to avoid using a one-size-fits-all approach to support, and instead take into account the specific needs of each child and their family. By meeting families where they are, and tailoring support accordingly, you can provide effective and meaningful assistance during this difficult time.

Type of loss

Children's grieving processes are uniquely shaped by the types of losses they experience. Losing someone to a long-term illness, a traffic accident, or suicide can bring about a range of difficulties and worries for the family. For instance, a child may be concerned about the possibility of the same thing happening to the other parent in the case of a car accident or a cancer diagnosis. Conversely, feelings of guilt are often a significant factor when it comes to suicide.

It is important to gain an understanding of the specific difficulties that may arise and tailor your support accordingly. However, we do well to note that the issues that are commonly associated with different types of loss may not always manifest in every case. As such, it's good to remain open-minded and enquire about any concerns before drawing conclusions.

The school's work with life-threatening illness and death

When a life-threatening illness or death occurs, there are several important tasks that the school should initiate. It can be challenging to know when a situation becomes serious enough for the school to take action during an illness. In the event of a death, you and the educational team may be so emotionally impacted that it can be difficult to respond appropriately and effectively. In the following sections, we will outline how the school can respond and highlight the tasks to manage during a life-threatening illness, after the death occurs, and in the following weeks and months.

Actions to take when encountering life-threatening illness

We have all experienced getting ill. Sometimes it's more serious than other times. However, for those around us, it can be challenging to determine when an illness becomes serious and requires urgent attention. The same is true when a family member of a pupil falls ill. It is not always easy to determine when the illness has become so serious that the school needs to respond. For the affected family, who are in a very stressful circumstances, the same can apply.

Our recommendation is that it is always best to contact the child's family as quickly as possible when you become aware of a potentially difficult family situation. This contact allows you to understand what is going on in the home and ensure that you can proactively support the pupil. For the family, it will be reassuring to know that the school is aware of the difficult life situation and is ready to help.

The first contact with a family affected by illness can be used to clarify the situation and establish a framework for ongoing communication between the school and home. This helps the school stay informed of any changes in the illness and respond appropriately. However, families may not always have the resources to provide regular updates, so it's important for the school to suggest a plan for communication that works for everyone. For example, the school could arrange to call every two weeks or when there is a significant change in the illness.

If there are multiple children in the family attending the school, it may be helpful to establish a shared form of communication. This can save the family time and ensure that all teachers are aware of any changes.

For serious illness, it is recommended to schedule a physical meeting between the school and the family. It can be beneficial to have two representatives from the school, such as a member of the leadership team or a colleague with experience in crisis situations. During the meeting, two key points should be addressed:

1. **Get permission to talk about the course of the illness.** It is important to recognize that as a school staff member, you cannot disclose a serious illness to a child if the parents have chosen to keep it a secret. We have been called to educational institutions several times when parents have chosen to keep an illness a secret, leading to great distress for the child. Even

if they don't know what it is, children can sense that something is wrong in the family, either because they overhear fragments of a conversation or simply due to their intuition. In such situations, the child is excluded from grieving with the family and must therefore worry alone.

Parents do not withhold information to harm their child, but because they want to protect them from the difficult truth. The consequence, however, is that the child loses trust in the adults around them because they deliberately hide what is going on. This applies not only to the parents but also to the pedagogical team, who know more than they say. We therefore always recommend that families be open with their children. If you come across a family where the course of illness is being kept hidden, it is important to talk to the parents about why they have chosen this approach and the problems that come with it.

Tell the parents about the distress you are perceiving within the child, so that they understand that silence does not help the child but is likely to harm them. Also tell the parents that you would like to have the opportunity to talk to the child about the course of the illness because you want to be an important support in a difficult time. Most families will listen and be forthcoming.

2. **Inform the family about how the school can assist them.** When a family is in crisis, daily life can become overwhelming and difficult to manage. Any support that the school and class community can offer can make a significant difference. However, families in crisis may not know what kind of support they need, and may struggle to answer questions like 'What can we do to help?' or 'What do you need?'

To overcome this challenge, it is important to consider in advance what specific support the school can offer. Would homework help be useful? Could a support person be assigned to assist the child? Could the school facilitate communication with other families or coordinate help from the class community, such as providing transportation to and from extracurricular activities? Offering concrete forms of support makes it much easier for the family to accept help during their difficult time.

By going through the two points above with the family, you establish a good starting point for your further work. It is also important to recognize that challenges can arise in relation to the child's well-being during the course of the illness. Worries and hospital visits can cause concentration problems and make it difficult to find time and energy for homework. It is not always possible to ignore all the difficulties that this life situation presents. Instead, it is about helping the child to cope with it. If there is a learning gap that arises during this process, this is something you can help the child catch up on later.

Actions to take when the death has just occurred

Communication is important between the family and the school when dealing with life-threatening illnesses. The school staff should be informed immediately when a death occurs so that they can offer support to the affected child and family. However, there are times when communication may not be effective, especially in cases of unexpected deaths such as car accidents or suicides. In such situations, it is the school's responsibility to reach out to the family and ask for confirmation about what has happened.

If there are rumours or posts on social media regarding a young person's death, it is essential to confirm the authenticity of the facts before taking any action. It is a really bad joke to write on Facebook that someone has died; we cannot be 100% sure that this is not the case until we have received oral or written verification from the affected family or another authority (such as the police).

Therefore, coordinate your efforts at the school and consider which person should contact the family in the situation. This is particularly relevant if there are several affected children in different classes, so that the family is not contacted by three different teachers who all want to know the same. Consider which person in the teaching team is best suited to make contact. The choice should be based on who is best equipped for the difficult conversation, but also who has the best relationship with the child and the family. This could be a class teacher, school support staff, or an educational psychologist. In the initial conversation, it is important to work though the following stages:

1. Establish contact with the family and confirm the situation.

2. Obtain permission from the family to disclose necessary facts to school personnel, other classmates, and their families.

3. Arrange for a later face-to-face meeting with the family to discuss the child's return to school, which will often be after the funeral.

4. Ensure ongoing communication between the school and the home.

It is important that, after the initial clarification, you pass on relevant information to colleagues and classmates. If this is not done, situations may arise where divergent stories and rumours spread. This creates confusion at the school, and it is uncomfortable for the affected family if they are confronted with false stories.

However, it is also important that the school does not disclose more than what has been verified by the family. If faulty information has been released by the school once, it creates mistrust and undermines credibility. It is better to explain that you still lack facts but are working to obtain it than to base explanations on secondary sources.

Always consider which information is relevant. It is not always beneficial to delve into the specifics of the death. If there are rumours circulating about the way the death occurred, for example after suicide or murder, providing additional context may be necessary. In such instances, it's vital to engage in a conversation with the parents or surviving parent, explaining the need for sharing more information. Consulting with a mental health professional could be a wise step in these situations. Rumours tend to spread swiftly, so providing honest and direct insight as soon as possible after a death often helps minimize speculation. With the initial information confirmed and passed on, it is important to prepare for welcoming the grieving pupil back to the class. Here, we recommend that you start with an initial conversation with the pupil and their family, preferably before they return to class.

This could be done during your visit to their home or on the first day the child returns to school. The goal of the conversation is to ensure basic rules for the near future. These give the pupil security about what will happen in a world that has suddenly become dramatically changed and uncertain with the loss. In cases of sudden deaths, you may find that the child is in a state of shock; here, it may be a good idea to simplify the conversation and focus on creating stability for them. The topics that are generally important to cover regarding the pupil's return are as follows.

1. **How do we tell the class about what happened?** Discuss how to best communicate what has happened to classmates, and who will take on the task. Have some suggestions as to how this can be done (you can explain, the pupil can explain, or you can explain together). This is important even if classmates and their parents have already been informed, as it creates a framework and a shared history for the class. At the same time, it is comforting for the grieving pupil to be present, so that they know and agree with the story being told. It is rarely a good idea to make an agreement *not* to explain anything. In part, it can be difficult for the pupil to hide that something is wrong, and there are often already rumours

circulating. Silence can increase the spread of rumours, and the class is then left to handle the loss without adult help. You may therefore need to insist that it be explained in the class, because some pupils already know something, and you also have a responsibility to the classmates.

2. **What does the pupil do if they get upset?** The grieving child rarely has previous experience with grief and can therefore be overwhelmed by their own often-unexpected reactions. What should they actually do if they suddenly get upset in the middle of a lesson? It can be difficult for the pupil to know what they are allowed to do. Can they leave the classroom, and can they take a friend with them? Should the teacher be told, or is it just something they do? Make agreements in advance about what the child is allowed to do if they get upset. Such frameworks ensure that they do not sit and feel trapped in the class if they suddenly feel bad. Make sure that such rules are passed on to all teachers in the class, including substitutes.

3. **Give the pupil an overview of how the school plans to handle their grief.** Losing a parent represents a huge loss of control. Therefore, it is important that the pupil regains a sense of being able to control elements in their own life. It can be difficult in an unfamiliar situation where all aspects of life are often affected by the loss. Give the child security by telling them precisely how the school plans to handle the loss. Present what you plan to do to help them in the short and long term, and give them the opportunity to object to initiatives they do not like, and to suggest changes or other approaches. It may be that the school sees an advantage in certain plans, but if the pupil does not like them, they are doomed to fail. Instead, spend time explaining to the pupil why you think a particular support initiative will be good

– and don't be afraid to bring it up later if the pupil initially declines it.

At the same time, ensure that regular meetings are scheduled where there is time to follow up on how things are going. Initially, it should be more frequent, but if the grieving pupil generally seems to thrive, you can increase the time interval between meetings. We suggest monthly meetings in the beginning, and if there are no major challenges, this can be changed to biannual or annual meetings. The meetings can be used to show that the school remembers the loss and takes the child's grief seriously. Use the time to check in and review any difficulties related to the pupil's learning and well-being in the class. End the meeting by setting a time for the next meeting.

As a teacher, it's not just important to support the grieving pupil; you also have a responsibility to ensure the well-being of the entire class. A grieving child's successful return to school largely depends on whether the class is ready to receive them. It's rare for classmates to have experience in supporting friends in grief, so they too need help understanding how to do so. Consider having conversations in the class about what it means to be a good friend when a classmate is in crisis. Ideally, such conversations would have taken place before, but if not, make sure to talk to the grieving pupil beforehand so they are prepared for the topic. Otherwise, it can feel like an ambush.

If the death occurred as a result of an accident or another situation that has gained press attention, it's important for the school to be prepared for the increased interest that may follow. In such cases, it may also be necessary to protect teachers, parents, and children from inquisitive journalists. There have been instances where the press showed up at schools unannounced and tried to interview pupils about a suspicious death. Therefore, it's important to consider who will handle press contact. The school principal is often a good choice since they typically have experience in dealing with media contacts.

Actions to take when a pupil dies from suicide

When a child dies from suicide the school must address the concerned pupils' need for information and care. Rumours of murder and speculations about the causes of the suicide, where other pupils may be accused of complicity, mean that school management must quickly plan what should be said, when, and to whom. This may require cooperation with the police, who have contact with the deceased's parents, so that accurate information is given that can dampen rumours in the school.

Here, the school's need to create calm can at times be complicated by adults' desire to keep information about the cause of death and the way it happened hidden. If the police have a good reason for why it's important to inform the school about this, it's usually accepted by the family. It can also ease the situation for siblings returning to school, as they don't have to deal with rumours if their classmates know the facts. Such situations require planning for information and care. An additional responsibility is to avoid romanticizing and unnecessary attention on the act of suicide, as it can increase the possibility of others seeking attention through a similar action. By highlighting the pain that suicide causes both for the family and friends left behind, the risk of this is reduced.

Action points in the aftermath of the loss

It is common to assume that the most difficult time for a grieving child is immediately following their loss, and that with time, all wounds will heal. However, this is rarely the case. Grief evolves and takes on new forms as people grow and discover new aspects of themselves. For instance, it is natural for a child to experience renewed grief when the deceased parent is absent for significant events or milestones, such as a graduation.

In this context, most children have both parents present, which can put the grieving child's loss into a new perspective. They may also experience renewed grief during events such as parent-teacher conferences, the anniversary of their parent's death, Christmas, or their own birthday. Immediately after the loss, it is advisable to provide the grieving child with some guidelines on what to do if they feel sad or need a break. This can give them a set of tools to use if they encounter difficulty. Here are some suggestions:

- Provide the child with a small electric candle they can turn on when they feel sad. The teacher can see it and respond accordingly. This works particularly well for young children at the beginning of primary school.

- Allow the child to leave the classroom to listen to music.

- Permit the child to leave the classroom with a friend.

- Provide the child with a specific teacher or support staff they can always talk to.

Grieving children often feel that their school and friends quickly forget their loss and return to normal everyday life, while they are still learning to cope with the loss. It can make a significant difference if, on special days, you remind the child that you also remember their family member who is missing, so they don't feel alone. On such days, it is important to provide space for the child to express their grief without feeling abnormal.

The school's support for grieving children

We recommend that schools make a structured response plan. Such a plan can help ensure that the necessary steps are taken when a child encounters critical illness or death in the family. Good questions to answer include:

- Who needs to be informed about the loss (staff, classmates, families)?

- What needs to be done now and what needs to be done later?

- How do we ensure good and ongoing communication with the family?

- How do we ensure that the child receives support tailored to personal needs?

For more guidance on how to support children at school, we recommend reading *Loss in the Family – A Reflection on How Schools Can Support Their Students* by A. Dyregrov and colleagues (2020b).

Conclusion

Supporting children who are grieving is not a one-off task, but rather a continuous process that requires ongoing attention and care. Although initial and targeted support is needed, it is equally important for schools to maintain their focus on a child's grief, even when things seem to be going well. As children continue to grow and learn new things about themselves and life, they will experience grief in new and unexpected ways. It is important that they do not feel alone with their memories and that schools remain aware of their circumstances of loss for as long as they are in their care.

As school staff, it can be challenging to know how far to go and what to ask when meeting with someone who is grieving. Our experience is that it's better to ask too many questions rather than too few. Families and children who are grieving need to be met by professionals who are not afraid to ask difficult questions. It is through these questions and good planning that you make a difference.

When working with children's grief, you may sometimes find that the support you try to provide is received incorrectly or has no effect. You may also encounter children who do not want to receive help. If this happens, consider why the help is not working. Is it because you don't have a good relationship? Is there another adult who has a better relationship with the child and can therefore provide better support? If this is not the case, can you identify the factors that prevent the child from opening up, and can you influence them? If things are so severe that community services need to be involved, forgive yourself, especially when a conversation doesn't go as you would like. Know that the work you do makes a difference in the child's life, and never be afraid to try again. Sometimes it just takes the courage to ask again or ask a question in an alternative way.

'I have a fantastic teacher. One that I can always talk to. He is really nice, and sometimes he has suggestions for what we can do. But I always get to decide for myself whether I think it's nice or not. I get to decide what I want.' *Tine, aged ten*

Chapter 11

Therapy with Children

Introduction

In this chapter, we primarily discuss how we and other professionals work with therapy for children with complicated grief. At the same time, we are keen that families receive early assistance after experiencing a death, especially if a parent or sibling has died. Good assistance for parents is essential in preventing or slowing the development of complicated grief in children. Children depend on adults – not only as role models and to provide information that helps them understand what has happened, but also for the reactions they are experiencing in themselves and others. Therefore, adult support that indirectly helps children makes sense.

For this reason, we first write about early intervention and then about therapy for children. However, it is important to point out that families' need for professional support is very individual. Many go through grief with their own resources and with support from their social network. Other families may benefit from one or two conversations to create good frameworks for their further processing of grief, while some families need more support and therapy, aimed at both the family as a whole and individual members. Often such needs also vary according to the type of loss the family has experienced. Research has shown that there is usually a need for more professional support after unexpected deaths (e.g., accidents or suicide) than in expected deaths (e.g., illness or old age) (Berg *et al.*, 2016; Niederkrotenthaler *et al.*, 2012).

This chapter is particularly relevant for professionals working with psychological and therapeutic interventions for grieving children. We present strategies that can make a difference both with early intervention and when grief becomes more complicated and requires special interventions. The goal is that after reading the chapter, you will have gained greater insight into various therapeutic support measures that can help children with complications in their grief.

Early intervention in families

In this section, we present two interventions used for families grieving after a death. The aim is to prevent problems in children by creating good communication and a warm family environment. In the US, psychiatrist Irwin Sandler and his colleagues have developed a programme to prevent problems in children who have lost parents. The Family Bereavement Program (FBP) has shown positive effects over a very long time, even into adulthood (Sandler *et al.*, 2018). The FBP works in small groups with both a parent and a child module, with weekly two-hour meetings over 12 weeks. Several families in the same situation meet during the process. Children and parents are together for four meetings. Each family receives a tailored programme according to their needs. Parents learn principles of so-called 'positive parenting', which is about developing good parent–child relationships. They learn how to do positive things together, develop good listening skills, spend time with each child individually, and learn how to see positive qualities in their children. Emphasis is placed on the importance of maintaining rules and discipline using what is called the three Cs: 'Be Clear, Be Calm, Be Consistent.' Children learn how to share their experiences and express their feelings, and are then met by parents who have learned to listen better.

Older children also learn how to appreciate the parents' efforts for the family. They choose positive things they can do together and talk about how to avoid conflicts and solve problems together. Children learn about good communication; the connection between stressful events, thoughts, and feelings; and how to counteract negative thoughts and misunderstandings. Problem-solving and re-formulation are included, and self-esteem and constructive thinking are worked on. Children discuss what they can take responsibility for in the family and what they cannot. In each meeting for children, 15 minutes are allocated for discussing grief-related feelings. Here, they can openly discuss topics such as anger, sadness, hiding feelings, and unusual grief experiences. A more detailed description of this programme can be found in Ayers and colleagues (2013).

Based on our experience with early intervention in grieving families over several decades at the Centre for Crisis Psychology in Bergen, we have developed a follow-up programme for families after the sudden death of a parent (e.g., following a car accident, suicide, sudden illness) (Pereira *et al.*, 2017). We also use this approach when we meet families soon after other types of death, such as a child's death.

1. In the first conversation, which takes place in the first few days after the loss, we provide brief psychoeducational information on sleep, participation in rituals, use of social networks, advice to parents on how to talk to children about the death, and advice on returning to nursery and school.

2. In the second conversation (during the first weeks), the focus is on a review of what happened, if possible with the whole family together, and the communication of new information so that children are well informed and can understand how and why the death occurred. There is discussion about both grief reminders and trauma reminders, and children and adults are given advice on how to be around each other. Self-help methods for reducing uncomfortable memories

that come unexpectedly, improving sleep, and reducing speculation and self-blame are also conveyed.

3. In the third session (5 to 7 weeks after the loss), trauma-specific methods can be used to reduce trauma-related distress that may still be present, so as not to hinder the natural grieving process. At this point, the conversation also focuses on finding a balance between letting go of the deceased and keeping their memory alive in their heart. If children or adults feel that they did not get a chance to say goodbye, they are encouraged to talk to the deceased in their imagination, to say what they did not have the opportunity to say. They can also write to them if they wish. The importance of finding a balance between spending limited periods of time close to the loss and taking breaks from grieving is emphasized.

4. In the fourth and fifth sessions (between 3–6 months and 12–13 months after the loss), the family discusses what has happened since the last session, and the focus is on how to live with grief over time. If thoughts of the deceased still occupy their minds, they are encouraged to go through and tidy up their belongings such as clothes, shoes, toys, and bedroom, adjust the number of visits to the grave, light candles less frequently, or reduce other ritual actions that make them more preoccupied with the deceased than with the life that now has to take on new routines. They are also encouraged to give themselves permission to grieve less. They should still keep the deceased in their hearts, but not let thoughts of them dominate. They can learn to set aside a specific time to approach the loss, and if thoughts come up outside this time, they can be postponed until the designated 'grief' time (see also Chapter 7, Coping with Loss). One topic in the sessions is how the family communicates about grief and how they support each other. The session close to the anniversary

summarizes the year that has passed, how it was on that day, and how they can live with the loss and grief going forward. If children or parents continue to struggle with grief to the point where it affects their daily functioning, therapy (as described later) is recommended.

We initiated a randomized controlled study of this approach for surviving parents and children after the death of the other parent, but had to abandon it due to recruitment problems. However, our interventions are in line with what experienced clinicians and researchers believe about early intervention, and what has been recommended by others (A. Dyregrov *et al.*, 2020a; Schonfeld *et al.*, 2016). For families in need of more follow-up, the number of sessions is increased or correspondingly decreased if close follow-up is no longer considered necessary.

In early intervention, it may be appropriate to see the family as a whole. Other times, it may be a teenager who separately needs to learn methods for meeting friends or managing school situations, or a parent who needs a counselling session because of concerns for the children. Some families require fewer hours, others more. Normally, family sessions are supplemented with parent sessions after a sibling's death. These are necessary because parents react differently, and the interaction between them must be taken into account. Examples of topics in such sessions include lack of understanding between them, mutual blame, and different opinions about what to say to the children (Ayers *et al.*, 2013). Parents and other caregivers are central in promoting adaptive grieving and preventing complicated grief (Alvis *et al.*, 2022).

Interventions for young children below the age of six aim at assisting parents and caretakers in being present and helpful for children. By informing and discussing children's reactions and coping mechanisms, emphasizing the need for open and honest communication with their young children, and ensuring that warmth is combined with discipline, these interventions can enable parental capacity to be upheld. There has been little research conducted on interventions for this age group, but readers may find a description of various studies in a systematic review carried out by Chen and Panebianco (2018). For therapy, these authors found play therapy and play-based activities most common. Psychoeducation and parent/family components were also included, helping children and parents to normalize reactions, express grief, and develop skills that promoted good communication and parent–child relationships.

Therapy for children with complicated grief

Despite early intervention, some children and families struggle with complicated grief reactions over time. This is especially true for children who have experienced suicide, murder, or accidents, but also for children who develop long-term problems after the death of a loved one due to illness. In the following section, we describe in more detail how to work with complicated grief reactions in therapy. Chapter 6, Complicated Grief Processes, describes some of the factors that indicate a referral to therapy for children and young people.

We often have parents (or surviving parents/caregivers) attending the first session when children are referred for complicated grief reactions. This usually provides comfort for most children. Gradually, parental presence can be reduced. Children can choose who they want to bring with them, and sometimes they like to bring a friend. We use a direct but respectful approach, so that the family gains a model for how to talk about difficult topics. In the first session, we map out how the death occurred, how much the children have been exposed to, and the reason for their referral to treatment. This creates a foundation for prioritizing what needs to be addressed first in therapy. We want to know what kind of relationship the child had with the person who died, what information the child has received, how the nursery or school has been informed, and how the family has communicated since the death.

What the children think about the future often provides a picture of potential future pessimism or optimism, as well as revealing the coping resources they have.

Children typically do not like long, intense conversations, and it is advantageous to use concrete methods that allow them to symbolize their grief through more creative expressions, as well as involving play, card games, or other stress-reducing activities in the conversations. We also sometimes have an initial conversation with the parents before the child is brought in. If a child has experienced many difficult situations in the past, we approach them cautiously and take time to build a relationship, being careful not to let the emotional intensity of the conversation become too great. We try to convey strategies early on that can help alleviate the most troublesome symptoms so that they feel a greater sense of control and hope that they can get better.

Treatment of complicated grief – research-based approaches

There are well-documented treatment methods for children with complicated grief. Most therapists use cognitive behavioural therapy (CBT) or conduct therapy in a group setting, and almost all will work early in therapy to reduce traumatic reactions that may disrupt the grieving process and integration of the loss, before grief becomes the central focus of the sessions (Cohen *et al.*, 2006; Cohen & Mannarino, 2011; Layne *et al.*, 2001; Spuij *et al.*, 2013). Boelen and co-workers (2021) were the first to show that a CBT programme can effectively reduce prolonged grief disorder symptoms up to a year after treatment. The treatment includes many of the elements described in this section of the book.

The work with complicated grief in children always involves psychoeducational information on grief and trauma reactions, establishment of a narrative of what happened, and clarification of any misunderstandings about the incident or their own reactions (cognitive restructuring). Conversations will focus on feelings of longing, guilt and self-blame, anxiety, and other emotional reactions, as well as support from others, handling of anniversaries, and expanding children's coping strategies. This helps to strengthen their ability to handle emotions while emphasizing the meaning of the event, and the loss for them, and their thoughts about the future. It is also important to help children find good ways to maintain a relationship with the deceased. In therapy, discussions will cover the death itself, any ambivalent feelings about the deceased, and positive memories, and will work on redefining the relationship with them.

Judith Cohen's model for the treatment of what she calls 'traumatic grief' includes most of the elements described above (Cohen et al., 2006; Cohen & Mannarino, 2011). Traumatic grief is the grief that occurs after a child has lost a loved one under traumatic circumstances that disrupt the normal grieving process (Cohen et al., 2004). Trauma processing is a key element in Cohen's initial sessions, with a focus on teaching children to handle both grief and trauma reminders. The treatment consists of 12–16 sessions with the child and 4 joint sessions with the parents. Although the treatment is described in a manual with structured guidance for the sessions, emphasis is placed on the therapist's creativity and flexibility so that the treatment can be tailored to the individual child. In the trauma component, the focus is on developing the child's skills in expressing emotions; handling stress; understanding the connection between thoughts, feelings, and behaviour; establishing their trauma history (narrative); and clarifying misconceptions.

The grief-focused components include talking about the loss and grief, addressing ambivalent feelings towards the deceased, holding on to positive memories, redefining the relationship with the deceased, and exploring how new relationships can be created and new meaning can be found in life. This approach has been shown to reduce complicated grief reactions.

Therapy for different types of complicated grief in children

As described in Chapter 6, Complicated Grief Processes, there are different forms of complicated grief in children. Children referred for treatment may have problems with suppressed or prolonged grief, separation anxiety, and managing specific grief reactions. We will present some examples of how we work with different types of complicated grief. Children's problems are often complex, as they may struggle with both prolonged grief and trauma reactions, and may also be very angry or have a strong sense of guilt. This means that all therapy is different and should reflect an assessment of what is most important to address.

Therapy for prolonged grief in children

In the context of working with children who struggle with strong, prolonged grief that does not subside over time and where thoughts still revolve around the deceased, the child learns strategies to take breaks from grief. This means that in defined, fixed periods of time during the day, preferably for no more than 15–30 minutes, they let their thoughts come very close to the one they have lost. They can do this in their own 'time of grief' or in the afternoon together with their father, mother, or sibling, where the family talks about the deceased. Depending on how much time they normally spend thinking about them, it may be necessary to set aside time every day at first, but gradually less often.

During the allocated time, children are encouraged to focus on their loss, look at pictures or use other concrete memories (clothing, jewellery, etc.) to get close to their emotions. They can think about what they liked best about the deceased, what he or she meant to them, what important things they learned from them, and so on. Children decide for themselves what they want to think about during this time, but many need examples of topics for this 'focus time' or 'grief time'. If there is a lot of unfinished business in the relationship with the deceased, for example if the death was sudden, suggest tasks such as: 'Imagine that in your thoughts you go to your mother/father before the death occurred and say what you wish you had had time to say. Maybe you can write it down?' If the child cannot write, an adult can help. Letter writing to the one they have lost can also be part of the time when they approach the loss. The complexity of the tasks they receive, of course, depends on their age and level of maturity.

In addition to this 'parent time' (or time with another family member/friend), the task is that when these thoughts or the sense of loss arise at any other time, they say to themselves: 'I will think about this in my parent time.' They must, therefore, 'postpone' their grief until the set time. They should be encouraged to do this every time, so the process becomes automatic and the thought is interrupted before it occupies their consciousness. It is important that they do not get annoyed with themselves or feel that they are doing something wrong if the thoughts come anyway. They just need to repeat to themselves that it should not be dealt with now. Worry postponement can therefore be used for thoughts that occupy attention (Wells & Sembi, 2004).

A 13-year-old girl came to therapy four years after her father's death. She thought about him all the time, even during school hours and afternoons, and missed him deeply. She worried about his absence in important moments of her life, such as academic achievements, marriage, and when she would become a mother and her father would have become a grandparent. Her grief had affected her daily life, and she would compare herself to her peers who had both parents. She kept a photo of her father on her nightstand, but had trouble sleeping and waking up because of it.

In her first therapy session, she learned the postponement worry exercise and imagined what her father would say about her constant grieving. With guidance, she learned to use her father as motivation to take breaks from her grief and imagine his encouragement for her to find joy in life. She quickly saw an improvement and continued with three more therapy sessions to talk about her father's significance in her life and how to keep his memory in a 'positive place'. She moved the photo to a different location and gathered meaningful objects associated with her father. She wrote down good memories and 'interviewed' family members about stories and facts about her father. She could 'go to this place' a few times a week to think about him. After therapy, she was no longer overwhelmed by grief but still missed her father sometimes.

Children who experience prolonged grief can benefit from resuming leisure activities and socializing with friends. They may feel guilty experiencing happiness that their loved one cannot share, but it's important to remind them that the deceased would have wanted them to be happy. Children may also feel more mature than their peers but need to understand that others may not fully comprehend their grief. It's helpful to advise them on how to communicate with their support network and not withdraw.

Therapy for grief where trauma dominates

When trauma reactions dominate grief, work is done with intrusive memories from specific episodes, such as those from the course of the illness, the moment of death, when they received the news of the death, or when they saw the deceased. In these cases, trauma therapeutic methods are used, which are specifically directed towards these problems. The strategy used will of course depend on whether it is intrusive memories, avoidance reactions, or strong activation/fear that dominate. The most common are intrusive memories, and we have previously described a number of different methods that can be used here (A. Dyregrov, 2010).

A 16-year-old girl discovered her father lying on the floor, injured and surrounded by a pool of blood. The traumatic event left an indelible mark, haunting her both during the day and at school, and especially at bedtime. To cope, the girl learned self-help techniques, including a screen technique where she actively manipulated the image, shrinking, enlarging, and altering the colour quality. In the second session, a combination of thought field therapy and eye movement desensitization and reprocessing (EMDR) further reduced the intensity and frequency of the haunting images. In later sessions, it was important to explore the father's significance in her life and address her fear of losing her mother. Gradually, the girl learned to accept that she couldn't control her mother's fate and that her mother must live her own life.

Therapy for family relationships that complicate grief

When complicated grief reactions arise because of various family relationships, a combination of family sessions and sessions with parents or the surviving parent is necessary. If parents withhold information from children, and they struggle to understand what has been happening (such as illness), it is important to explain to the adults how this creates problems for the children. Sometimes it is obvious that children will want to know more about what the adults know about the death or what the deceased looked like. Both after suicide and murder, adults may withhold information to protect the children, who then supplement with their own imagination. The therapist can ensure that correct facts and advice are provided, tailored to the children's age and maturity. If the parents have not told the correct version of how the death occurred, for example that the person died of a heart attack when it was suicide, or have withheld information, the parents are helped to explain why they chose to do as they did – but thereafter they must be completely honest.

Certain families struggle so intensely after a death that more systematic family work is necessary. This may be because children are unnecessarily burdened with adult tasks, or conflicts arise between siblings or between adults and children.

> A father died suddenly and unexpectedly. Two children aged 14 and 16 lost the person who had taken on most of the caregiving responsibilities. He had provided them with support, comfort, and encouragement through text messages, and was always there for them when life wasn't easy. His role had been built over a long period of time.
>
> After his death, their mother tried to 'take over' this role without gradually gaining their confidence and trust over time. Her two teenage children pushed her away. Her fumbling attempts to take over only triggered a greater sense of loss of the father in the children. A series of family conversations and some conversations with the mother alone were necessary to address the situation. During these conversations, expectations were clarified, the situation was put into words, and gradually a 'ceasefire' and a cautious rebuilding of new trust was established. The family was given homework to spend time on activities together at home, and efforts were made to create more direct communication between the mother and her children about how they were all coping with the new situation they now had to learn to live with.

Therapeutic family work begins with an assessment of what the family is struggling with. Each member is given the opportunity to talk about the illness/death, while the therapist gains insight into both common and different coping and communication styles within the family, and how each individual relates to the illness or death and each other's grief. By listening to the family's account of what has happened, it is noted whether there is one person who 'owns' the story, or whether they build temporal and causal connections together. Unity and conflict within the family are mapped as a basis for what needs to be done next:

- Do they listen to each other?

- Do they only talk superficially about the death?

- Are there obvious gaps in the story and adults who are only slightly attentive to the children's needs?

- Does the family exhibit avoidance and little support for each other, requiring family members to develop better ability to collaborate and be a team?

- To what extent do they share thoughts, feelings, and facts?

Both strong and weak sides are mapped out before a proposal is agreed about what to focus on. An Australian research group led by David Kissane has provided valuable contributions on how therapeutic work in families can be conducted (Masterson *et al.*, 2013).

If conversation within the family has ceased or if children have taken on a caregiving role for their parents, communication (or the lack of it), and the redistribution of roles within the family become topics for discussion. Mutual accusations or blame between family members must be met with good family conversations, where the children's voices are heard, and the therapist creates space for everyone's contribution.

Therapy for supressed grief

Supressed grief is common in children and adolescents and can lead to complicated grief. As this coping mechanism keeps the emotional pain at bay, motivation is needed to open up and approach the grief closely. In a Chinese study (Li *et al.*, 2023), almost all of 44 interviewed adolescents and young adults never shared grief with family members. They held back tears during the funeral, pretended to have no grief after the loss, and kept grief secret (abiding by the 'family rules'). The authors comment on how the family climate of non-disclosure is due to a desire to protect the family in crisis. It is important to explain why it can be helpful to approach the loss and pain, and how to move forward together. We need to motivate families to do just that. This requires us to explain it in such a way that they trust us and are willing to approach the pain of loss and follow the advice we give them. Here is an example of how we address this in the conversation.

I understand that you may not want to think about or talk about what happened. Some people feel this way because they're afraid that they'll become too sad, be unable to stop crying, or will never feel happy again. It's natural to fear painful emotions, but we have emotions for a reason, even the difficult ones. If we constantly try to avoid them, we become exhausted, and this can make things worse. The brain uses a lot of energy to suppress thoughts and emotions without us even realizing it. You may notice this when your schoolwork becomes more difficult due to a decrease in concentration and memory, which affects your ability to learn.

I understand from your mum that you're having a hard time in school and have been withdrawing from your friends. I believe this may be related to the loss of your father, although I cannot be certain. I want you to know that it is possible to feel better, but it may require you to confront the grief and it may feel heavier before it starts to improve. It's important to remember that we don't have to be sad all the time, even after experiencing a loss. As psychologists, we know that emotions can be difficult and draining, but they're not dangerous. It's good to take breaks from the pain and search for positive emotions. In the end, positive emotions are the ones that prevail. If we suppress our negative emotions completely, we may struggle to experience positive emotions as well. However, by gradually approaching and working through our difficult emotions, we can eventually reach a point where we are able to experience more positive emotions.

The work on motivation in the first few conversations helps family members better understand why we are asking them to do what they would prefer to avoid. We try to create understanding of why it is important to approach the loss and how it can be done in a careful way so that they do not lose control. This means that the fear of losing control is explicitly addressed before we work on allowing them to approach the loss. We proceed carefully, and gradually advance towards the difficult emotions. We talk about one thing at a time, not for too long, and we explain that experiencing a feeling does not mean that they're losing control, but that they can approach their loss and quickly move away again. We show them how it is possible to think about something sad and then use a distraction that reduces the feeling, so they feel that they can have control and become less afraid to approach their loss.

In this work, we use different methods to expose emotions. It can involve bringing things into the conversations that are associated with the deceased, looking at pictures and videos of them, asking them to listen to music that they liked, and visiting places that have symbolic meaning, such as a favourite place they visited with their loved one. We ask them to say what happened when the person died and how they found out, but without too many details at first – then later more detailed. When the tolerance for grief and pain has increased, we can also use phrases that bring the loss to life, such as 'she is gone forever', and we can ask them to say these words out loud. Realization can also happen by going through reports, talking to medical or rescue personnel, and visiting the place of death (although this should be done with good preparation).

These methods make the loss more real, and they gradually open up channels for emotions. Children are prepared that they may become more upset at first because they are now willing to approach what has happened, but at the same time, they gain more control because they do not flee from their feelings. It is important to praise them for coping with this, and parents are also encouraged to give a positive response but leave the 'exposure' to the therapist so that it does not become too much. A joint conversation with parents can clarify how a child wants to handle conversations at home. Between sessions, children receive homework where they approach the deceased in thoughts or actions for a limited period, for example through writing assignments. Ritual acts also make the loss more real, for example where children and parents go together to the grave and light candles while the children tell the deceased, out loud or inside or through drawings, what they meant to them. Participating in a grief group can mean that they feel less alone, and they can meet other children who show how they manage their feelings.

When children use a high degree of suppression, they may refuse to speak with a psychologist. We advise parents to encourage their children to attend at least one therapy session, and promise them that the therapist will do the speaking and that they do not have to share anything they don't want to. It is then the therapist's job to tell stories about other children who have had similar experiences, how they coped with their situation, and what they did to feel better. These stories should be based on our experience but can be tailored to the child by choosing examples that are most similar to their own situation. Eventually, they may recognize their own experience in the stories and begin to engage in conversation. This approach makes it easier to convince the child to attend future therapy sessions. However, in some cases, we may need to wait for them to become older and realize that they need to seek help themselves.

Therapy for other types of complicated grief in children

When a child experiences persistent anger, guilt, or worry/anxiety after a death, it is important to first determine if this is a new issue that has arisen after the death or a worsening of an already existing clinical problem. The methods chosen should be effective in addressing the current problem. At the same time, it is important to discuss the death because there is often a connection between it and the emotional reaction.

Children who lose parents or siblings may develop separation anxiety, where they become highly dependent on being close to (and having control over) their parents or the surviving parent. This can become so limiting that it requires therapeutic help. Often, it reflects a strong fear that something will happen to others in the family. Calm conversations about this can help, while also training the child to gradually be further away from the parents. For some, the first step may simply be to be in a different room from the adults. To endure the greater distance, it may be helpful for the child to say calming phrases aloud to themselves, such as 'I can handle this', 'Nothing is going to happen', 'Mum is safe', and so on. This can also be combined with breathing techniques for relaxation. Another type of worry can be seen in children who become afraid of dying from the same illness as their parent, and they may require good information from health professionals and the use of the earlier mentioned methods to reduce worries (e.g., postponement worry exercise).

If guilt is the dominant emotion, a technique called Socratic thinking can be used. This challenges children's thoughts through simple questions that expand the perspective of their thoughts or actions. Alternatively, trauma therapy methods such as EMDR can be used to create movement in the rigid thoughts and emotions. With this method, children visualize the guilt or the central traumatic memory from the death, while receiving bilateral brain stimulation, usually by following the therapist's hand moving back and forth in their field of vision. A more detailed description of EMDR can be found in Shapiro and Laliotis (2011), and its efficacy with children is explored in Manzoni *et al.* (2021). For anger, various methods that emphasize putting words and expressions to the anger through conversation, writing, play, or drawing can be used.

If grief manifests itself through physical symptoms while a child is otherwise functioning well, it is natural to assume that it is related to repressed grief and unexpressed emotions. Once it has been determined that the symptoms are not due to an actual physical illness, our working hypothesis will be that the child needs to confront the loss, and that the same working method used for supressed grief can be applied. The therapist can explain to them that at times, the body expresses difficulties through pain and discomfort, and that it needs to be expressed through words and emotions. It is important to be aware that if the death was due to an illness, the child may be afraid that there is something seriously wrong with their own body, causing them to believe that they may also die. In this case, they will need reassurance about the tests that have been done and how stress can also cause physical symptoms.

In the clinic, we also receive referrals for children and young people who have begun to regulate physical tension after a death through self-harm (Bylund-Grenklo *et al.*, 2014). Here, we work to teach them other ways to manage tension, such as expressive and breathing techniques that they can use until the tension subsides. More mindfulness-inspired techniques, where they simply notice the tension, can also be used.

Conclusion

In this chapter, we have explored the various forms of complicated grief in children and the different ways to address them. Unlike adults, they tend to suppress their reactions and may be unwilling to discuss them. It can be difficult to distinguish between normal grief and complicated grief in children, but if a child is experiencing social difficulties, disengaging from their usual leisure activities, and showing persistently poor academic performance, it is cause for concern. In such cases, it is important to refer them for treatment and tailor the treatment to their specific difficulties without delay. However, motivating children to seek help can be difficult, even with effective treatment methods available. Collaboration between parents, educators, psychologists, and other important adults in the child's life is often necessary.

For therapists, we hope this chapter has provided some insight into the methods and therapies that we have found to be effective and useful in helping children with complicated grief reactions, based on our research and clinical experience.

Chapter 12

Disasters, Terror, and Children's Grief

Introduction

Disasters are often what are referred to as 'transnational', meaning that they can affect people from many different nations at the same time. In modern society, there are always families travelling who may be impacted by a disaster or a terrorist attack. Many have lost their lives, for example during the Southeast Asian tsunami, in terrorist attacks, and in major transportation accidents. Furthermore, refugees and asylum seekers have experienced loss during wars, armed conflicts, terrorist acts, political violence, torture, mass accidents, and natural disasters. Such events contain many traumatizing elements. Pandemics are a disaster not initially caused by humans, but the death tolls still reflect human choices regarding the handling of infection risks. Grief during pandemics can be negatively affected as restrictions can disrupt rituals and make social support more unavailable.

When children and young people experience a significant event, it can be quite challenging to distinguish which of their reactions are due to the loss, and which are due to other stressors and changes they may experience. If a child is the only survivor of the event, this is particularly difficult. After an earthquake, a child may have not only lost their loved ones but also survived extreme danger, seen their home or shelter destroyed, been forced to live in a tent in a totally changed environment, experienced aftershocks, not had their basic needs met, and so on. This is true too for refugees who have experienced war and displacement. Loss is a part of many changes in a child's life. The more stressors they experience during and after the loss, the greater the risk that their daily functioning will be affected (Layne *et al.*, 2014). Certain major events involve threats and dangers that persist over time, where so much happens around the death that it can affect both grief and a child's normal development. If many people die at the same time, even the networks that otherwise support a child may be affected and become more inaccessible. Similarly, circumstances like pandemics can make it difficult to provide support (even if it is available), because, for example, people cannot meet physically. Therefore, a disaster can lead to more complicated grief processes and make it difficult to support a child if society is fully or partially shut down.

In this chapter, we will address grief after deaths from major accidents or disasters, including terrorism.[1] Despite the fact that there are not many children who lose their loved ones in this way, major events are notable because many people can lose a loved one at the same time, and because the events receive significant media attention. However, the attention (or 'noise') around the events can disrupt grief. Our goal is for you to gain greater insight into what is unique about grief management after disasters and how it is possible to work with grief when so many people are affected at the same time.

---

1   Terrorism and large-scale accidents are both classified as disasters. These events share the common feature of affecting many individuals. Furthermore, addressing such incidents requires action at multiple levels, and places significant demands on leadership and organization. For further information, see A. Dyregrov (2018) and A. Dyregrov *et al.* (2019).

Exposure and reactions

Terrorism and disasters often involve exposure to life-threatening situations and violent losses, particularly in human-made disasters (e.g., terrorism and mass murder), but also in certain natural disasters such as earthquakes, landslides, and avalanches, where there are few or no warnings. These events can cost many lives, leave victims severely injured and mutilated, cause survivors and the bereaved to experience intense sensory impressions, and make hospital visits to see the deceased and attend funeral rituals difficult or requiring adjustment. In incidents involving a large number of deaths, such as pandemics, it may be necessary to forgo or limit normal farewells, funerals, and memorial services, which can have a negative impact on other people's ability to express participation and support.

The concepts used to describe grief after such incidents, such as 'traumatic grief', reflect the strong traumatic aspect involved. This means that children (as well as adults) continue to live with many trauma reminders related to the death and its circumstances, and the grief of both children and their caregivers can become complicated. Major events also result in intense media exposure and often involve legal proceedings and investigations. Bereaved individuals who are exposed to significant media coverage over time experience more grief (Brown & Goodman, 2005). The combination of grief and trauma can be especially difficult in major events, and follow-up in relation to the affected individuals must take into account the many legal and political processes that affect both the bereaved and survivors.

A child's loss of a loved one in a major event is a risk factor for the development of trauma symptoms and other mental health problems across cultures (Dawson *et al.*, 2014; Liu *et al.*, 2011; Usami *et al.*, 2014). What has received the most attention among researchers is how loss affects depression and post-traumatic stress reactions. In a meta-analysis of risk factors following natural disasters, grief was one of the factors most important in predicting depression (Tang *et al.*, 2014). Similarly, a number of studies have shown that children who lose loved ones in disasters have more problems in several areas than children who survive but do not lose anyone (Dawson *et al.*, 2014; Goenjian *et al.*, 2009; Kalantari & Vostanis, 2010; Pfefferbaum *et al.*, 2006).

Eighteen months after the terrorist attack on Utøya in Norway, where 69 young people were killed, 75% of bereaved siblings were above the level indicating complicated grief (K. Dyregrov *et al.*, 2014). Their levels of symptoms in other areas, such as post-traumatic stress reactions and general psychological distress, were also high and correlated with grief reactions. About half of the bereaved siblings had significant functional impairment and struggled with academic difficulties in school.

Children's reactions vary greatly depending on the type of disaster, the number of deaths, the care environment, and other aspects of the event. Although we do not have many studies that follow children over time and examine the paths of grief, we can generally say that disasters and terrorism have great potential to create various difficulties for children that last over time, especially after man-made events. If the child experiences personal danger and strong sensory impressions or creates fantasies about what happened to the person or people they lost, it can disrupt normal grief. Therefore, it is important to clarify what the child has been exposed to during the event, such as personal danger, strong sensory experiences, the reactions of others, and so on.

Intervention following disasters

Many of the interventions described for support after individual deaths are also important after a major event. This includes providing open and honest explanations to children, emphasizing that surviving parents are role models, teaching them how to communicate openly with children, and providing early and ongoing help. Because disasters are frightening and attract a lot of media attention, it is important to quickly create a safe environment for children as far as is possible, and to provide a lot of physical contact and assurances of adult presence and support. Both in the context of terrorism and natural disasters, parents and children can become separated. If this happens, reuniting them to ensure that children experience security should be a high priority.

At the same time, major events place great demands on both emergency personnel and the healthcare system. Many people need to be informed, and access to the facts may be limited at first, while later there may be a lot of information and rumours that need to be managed. Early on, there must be an overview established of, among other things:

- the number of affected or impacted children and their whereabouts

- which childcare institutions have been affected

- who the caregivers are in the children's environment or network

- who will take responsibility for a child if both parents have died

- measures to ensure the establishment of contact in the local community

- what information needs to be collected and then communicated to children and young people.

(A. Dyregrov, 2018, p.186)

This overview is used to plan and prioritize what needs to be done. Soon after a major incident, there is a need to organize evacuation and family assistance centres, meetings with emergency personnel and police, as well as aid to the injured, who may have also lost someone. Major incidents require organization and handling of groups of people, while the content of the direct support to those affected follows what has been written about in other chapters (e.g., in Chapters 8 and 10). The aid must be tailored to the situation at hand, but regardless, early support and information for parents, surviving parents, or caregivers responsible for the children will increase the chances that they will handle the situation well. Points for parents or other caregivers to take note of include:

- Children have an increased need for closeness and contact.

- Children should be allowed to participate in rituals, including memorial services.

- It is normal for children to experience various reactions such as sadness, anxiety, anger, self-blame, and so on after a disaster.

- Parents should share their thoughts and not hide their feelings from their children, but give word to them. If their reactions continue to be intense over time, others should step in for the children. Whatever the case, the strong reactions of both parents and others, witnessed by children, should be explained so they are understandable.

- Parents should accept children's need to talk, ask questions, or otherwise express what they have experienced.

- Adults should know that children, especially younger ones, may repeat the event in play, drawing, or action, and they should be allowed to do so.

- Children need assurances of the safety of their parents or the surviving parent, and that they will be there.

- The children's school should be contacted early on so that the staff are aware of the situation.

(A. Dyregrov, 2018, p.188)

Grief interventions in the aftermath of a major event

Disasters come in different forms and magnitudes, and studies on grief interventions reflect the diverse ways in which healthcare systems provide follow-up care across various countries.

Often in western culture, children are increasingly included in ritualistic activities to help them comprehend the reality of what has happened and to provide them with an opportunity to bid farewell while experiencing support from their environment. Children require guidance before, during, and after such events, to help them cope with their emotions. In cases where major events cause catastrophic damage, such as plane or helicopter crashes, the deceased might not be found intact, or at all. Nevertheless, memorial services and funerals serve as an essential part of the grieving process, even when the children cannot see the deceased. In situations where the dead are not found, a symbolic 'grave' may still hold significance, serving as a place for ritual actions and visits on commemorative days. In the aftermath of disasters, people who have lost loved ones, including children, may create fantasies about the deceased, such as how they died and the extent of their injuries. However, they do not need to receive horrifying details. It is important to provide concrete facts to counterbalance fantasies. Furthermore, our clinical experience has shown that seeing severely injured people can help in dampening such fantasies.

Following a major disaster, we were contacted by a family who had lost a loved one. Their two teenage children were struggling with constantly changing fantasies about the appearance of their deceased family member. These fantasies were even worse than the reality of the situation. We advised the family to contact the police, who had identified the person, in order to get a concrete image of their loved one's appearance. While we warned the family that the reality might be difficult to see, we explained that it would be helpful in reducing the children's constantly changing and distressing fantasies. The family later reported that although

> it was difficult to see, obtaining a clear image of their loved one's
> appearance helped to reduce their children's distressing fantasies.

Visiting the site of a traumatic event can be a meaningful and important experience for children to gain a better understanding of what happened and the circumstances surrounding it. It provides them with a visual representation of the event that can aid their comprehension. However, it is best that children are prepared and accompanied by trusted adults or staff who can provide simple explanations about what happened. Being on site also allows for a ritualistic farewell, which gives children the opportunity to say goodbye and leave flowers or other tributes. This can be a helpful step in their grieving process. However, in the case of extensive and sudden events, such rituals are often not possible. In some cases, such as ship accidents, throwing flowers into the sea can be a way to express grief. It is essential to suggest different ways for children to express their emotions. According to research after the terrorist attack on 22 July, young people who visited Utøya found the experience significant but more burdensome than adults (Kristensen et al., 2017).

In many countries, there are well-developed plans in place that include how to mobilize a response from healthcare personnel promptly to provide effective, immediate support in emergency situations. In some countries, like Norway, there is a tradition of holding information meetings and presentations specifically designed for children in the aftermath of a crisis. During joint gatherings for families, there are also presentations tailored to the needs of children.

Following the Utøya terrorist attack, four meetings were organized for the bereaved, with 200–250 participants attending within the first two years. These meetings included expert presentations in plenary sessions, psychoeducational sessions to provide participants with self-help methods, and small group meetings to connect parents with other parents and children with other children.

The self-help methods offered support in gaining a sense of control and coping with the trauma. Plenary sessions offered valuable advice from the inquiry commission about preparing for the trial and the anniversary, as well as short lectures on grief and grief management (A. Dyregrov et al., 2016).

Children and young people participated in small groups and activities were tailored to their specific age groups. These groups provided a safe environment to process different aspects of their loss and share experiences about what was helpful for them. Meetings were also organized to present children's experiences and questions to parents, enabling them to plan for the future together. Various forms of expression were utilized, and young people were encouraged to support and learn from each other.

In recent years, interventions based on cognitive behavioural psychology have become especially prevalent in cases where treatment has been necessary. When addressing major events that involve both trauma and loss, follow-up care must consider both (Cohen et al., 2004; A. Dyregrov et al., 2015b; Layne et al., 2008; Salloum & Overstreet, 2008).

To reach as many children as possible, many disaster relief efforts have utilized schools. However, this approach assumes that schools are intact or can be re-established in a new location. After school shootings, school terror, and natural disasters such as earthquakes, children may be reluctant to return to school. Despite this, it is important to prioritize getting them back to school quickly. If the school is destroyed or inaccessible, schooling can be arranged in tents or temporary structures.

Stability in everyday life and coverage of children's primary needs are essential for successful grief work. In certain natural disasters, such as those involving flooding or landslides, this stability can be difficult to maintain. If a child has lost a close family member, it is important to ensure early continuity in contact with parents or surviving guardians, a network of friends, and school. If a deceased parent was solely responsible for their child, and it takes a long time for the child to establish a close relationship with another responsible individual, the child may be at risk for negative consequences.

Information for bereaved adults and children should provide a comprehensive overview of the facts, as well as a better understanding of their own and others' reactions (A. Dyregrov & Kristensen, 2020).

> Following a landslide that struck a neighbourhood in Bergen, Norway, and resulted in fatalities and significant property damage, the city authorities organized factual sessions for adults. These sessions covered topics such as safety measures and alternative housing options. However, it was also necessary to hold two separate meetings for parents to discuss how best to support their children in the aftermath. During these meetings, parents expressed concern about their children's exposure to online coverage about the landslide. It became evident that it would have been beneficial to organize separate information sessions for children, providing them with the same facts as the adults, in order to ease their anxiety.

In the aftermath of significant events, providing information to children can help them prepare for the common reactions they may experience or witness in others. Additionally, they can learn techniques to manage physical arousal and prevent the development of traumatic stress symptoms. In situations where multiple children have died or been killed simultaneously, group discussions, with school classes for example, should be held to provide support to the children.

Group discussions with children

Much of the advice on discussions with children described in this chapter is versatile and can be applied to different contexts, including situations where children have lost a close friend or have experienced a frightening event together. The chapter devotes significant attention to this topic because it provides a valuable opportunity for children to process their experiences, share their feelings, and receive support from their peers.

In a group setting, children can articulate different aspects of their experience, gain insights from others, and have their emotions validated. It also allows them to build a more comprehensive understanding of the events and learn how to cope with any lingering effects such as intrusive memories and sleep disturbances.

Ideally, such a conversation should be led by two adults, one of whom should already be familiar to the children, such as a teacher. The session should last at least two hours and be limited to school-age children. The structure of the conversation can follow six steps: introduction, facts, thoughts, reactions, information, and ending.

During the *introduction*, the leaders should introduce themselves and explain the purpose of the meeting and the ground rules for the conversation. These rules should include respecting each other's privacy, waiting one's turn, and acknowledging that participation is voluntary.

Any new *facts* about what happened are shared with the group before allowing the children to say what happened or how they found out about it. Often, the children have slightly different pieces of information, which they share, so the group as a whole gets a better overview of the sequence of events. Misunderstandings and confusion can be clarified, so they have a common basis for understanding what happened. The review of facts provides insight into what the children have been exposed to and is important for planning further follow-up.

Questions about what the children were thinking (*thoughts*) during the incident or when they heard about it often automatically lead to answers where the children speak about their reactions and impressions. Therefore, there is a smooth transition from thoughts to *reactions*. It is wise to avoid questions such as 'How did you feel when you heard about it?' because it seems to hinder the conversation more than promote it. The question 'What do you remember best about what happened?', on the other hand, provides good information about their reactions and impressions, while allowing the children to talk about what is important to them.

If all the children witnessed someone's death or found someone dead, they can put words to the impressions they are left with. Impressions described with words contribute to the incident being more easily transferred to long-term memory and not remaining as fragments that push for space in consciousness. When children put words to impressions and reactions, the group leader can ask, 'Were there others who experienced it the same way?' Thus, the children hear that others have similar experiences to their own, and they have their thoughts and reactions confirmed and normalized.

Children can also be encouraged to write down their thoughts, or they can be given the task of completing sentences such as: 'The first thing I thought when I heard about what happened was...', 'The worst thing about what happened is that...', 'The impression that sticks most with me is...', and, 'I feel most upset when I think about...'

It is necessary to emphasize that the goal is not to elicit strong reactions from the group – what is important is that children hear that others may have thought and reacted as they have. Strong reactions can easily spread, and it requires a calm and reassuring demeanour from the adults to avoid this, with support and comfort that can calm them down.

Later in the conversation, the group leader(s) can bring together the threads of what the children have spoken about, point out similarities in their thoughts and reactions, and emphasize the normalcy of what they are experiencing (*information*). At the same time, leaders can talk about other children who have spoken about the same or similar reactions in similar situations. Children can gain insights into common reactions, but in such a way that they do not believe they *must* have these specific reactions to be 'normal'. Intrusive memories, triggers, fear and anxiety reactions, anger, revenge thoughts, sadness, guilt, and self-blame can be briefly mentioned.

It is also useful to know that such an event can weaken concentration and memory for a period, in case they later struggle with this. Children can be advised too on what they can do to better handle what has happened, for example:

- Talk to parents/surviving parent about what happened.
- Talk to friends about it.
- Visit the gravesite.
- Gather more information about the event.
- Write poems, keep a diary, and so on.

Towards the end of the conversation, ask the children if they have any questions or if anything is unclear, and you can ask them too how they experienced the meeting (*ending*). Praising participation is also part of the ending.

Follow-up over time

What needs to be done for children over time after major events depends heavily on what has happened, what the children have experienced, and how grief develops. If trauma reactions continue to be strong after more than a month, it is important to provide individual or group support to help them gain control of their reactions. This will allow the grieving process to proceed as smoothly as possible. Modern trauma therapy has proven effective, and children should not have to needlessly struggle with memories that still haunt them, strong avoidance reactions, or a nervous system that keeps them constantly on guard. If children are very concerned that other loved ones will die they may withdraw from friends and family, or experience strong guilt or anger, and it is essential to establish professional follow-up without delay.

Determining when to initiate therapy for complicated grief, as we described in Chapter 6 (Complicated Grief Processes), can be a challenge. However, the same principles apply after disastrous events. If children who have experienced loss live in close proximity to one another, they can benefit greatly from meeting others who are in a similar situation. Few people can understand their experience in the same way as those who have also lost loved ones in the same event. By connecting with those who share their experience, children can feel a sense of normalcy and belonging.

Society can play a role in facilitating this connection, for example by organizing events for families during the first year. These initiatives can provide a valuable foundation for coping. Nurseries and schools also have a responsibility to provide support for children and young people. We have summarized strategies that may be implemented from the school's perspective in Chapter 11, Therapy with Children, as well as elsewhere (A. Dyregrov *et al.*, 2015b). In addition, Turunen and Punamäki (2014) have provided practical suggestions on psychosocial support based on experience from school shootings in Finland.

Conclusion

Although not everyone needs therapeutic assistance, many children are deeply affected by terrorist and catastrophic events. This is especially true for those who lose a family member or friends, or who witness a death and experience strong sensory impressions. Therefore, it is essential to have good plans in place that screen children at various times after the event, so that the need for follow-up can be identified. This enables them to receive early help for post-traumatic stress reactions and, if they develop, complicated grief reactions. By providing appropriate support, we can help children cope with the aftermath of traumatic events and move forward in a healthy way.

References

Agid, O., Shapira, B., Zislin, J., Ritsner, M., *et al.* (1999). Environment and vulnerability to major psychiatric illness: A case control study of early parental loss in major depression, bipolar disorder and schizophrenia. *Molecular Psychiatry*, 4(2), 163–172.

Alahakoon, D. T. D. (2018). Childhood bereavement following parental death. *International Journal of Scientific and Research Publications (IJSRP)*, 8(8), 478–483.

Alvis, L., Zhang, N., Sandler, I. N., & Kaplow, J. B. (2022). Developmental manifestations of grief in children and adolescents: Caregivers as key grief facilitators. *Journal of Child & Adolescent Trauma*, 16(2), 446–457. https://doi.org/10.1007/s40653-021-00435-0.

American Psychiatric Association (2022). *Diagnostic and Statistical Manual of Mental Disorders* (DSM-5-TR). Arlington, VA: American Psychiatric Association. https://doi.org/10.1176.

Appel, C. W., Johansen, C., Christensen, J., Frederiksen, K., *et al.* (2016). Risk of use of antidepressants among children and young adults exposed to the death of a parent. *Epidemiology* (Cambridge, MA), 27(4), 578–585.

Ariès, P. (1981). *The Hour of Our Death*. New York, NY: Alfred A. Knopf.

Asgari, Z. & Naghavi, A. (2020). The experience of adolescents' post-traumatic growth after sudden loss of father. *Journal of Loss and Trauma*, 25(2), 173–187.

Ayers, T. S., Wolchik, S. A., Sandler, I. N., Twohey, J. L., *et al.* (2013). The Family Bereavement Program: Description of a theory-based prevention program for parentally-bereaved children and adolescents. *OMEGA – Journal of Death and Dying*, 68(4), 293–314.

Balk, D. E., Zaengle, D., & Corr, C. A. (2011). Strengthening grief support for adolescents coping with a peer's death. *School Psychology International*, 32(2), 144–162.

Berg, L., Rostila, M., Saarela, J., & Hjern, A. (2014). Parental death during childhood and subsequent school performance. *Pediatrics*, 133(4), 682–689.

Berg, L., Rostila, M., & Hjern, A. (2016). Parental death during childhood and depression in young adults – A national cohort study. *Journal of Child Psychology and Psychiatry*, 57(9), 1092–1098.

Bergman, A.-S., Axberg, U., & Hanson, E. (2017). When a parent dies – A systematic review of the effects of support programs for parentally bereaved children and their caregivers. *BMC Palliative Care*, 16(1), 39. https://doi.org/10.1186/s12904-017-0223-y.

Boelen, P. A., Spuij, M., & Reijntjes, A. H. A. (2017). Prolonged grief and posttraumatic stress in bereaved children: A latent class analysis. *Psychiatry Research*, 258, 518–524.

Boelen, P. A., Lenferink, L. I. M., & Spuij, M. (2021). CBT for prolonged grief in children and adolescents: A randomized clinical trial. *American Journal of Psychiatry*, 178(4), 294–304. https://doi.org/10.1176/appi.ajp.2020.20050548.

Bonanno, G. A. (2021). The resilience paradox. *European Journal of Psychotraumatology*, 12(1), 1942642. https://doi.org/10.1080/20008198.2021.1942642.

Bowlby, J. (1963). Pathological mourning and childhood mourning. *Journal of the American Psychoanalytic Association*, 11(3), 500–541.

Brent, D., Melhem, N., Donohoe, M. B., & Walker, M. (2009). The incidence and course of depression in bereaved youth 21 months after the loss of a parent to suicide, accident, or sudden natural death. *American Journal of Psychiatry*, 166(7), 786–794.

Brent, D., Melhem, N., Masten, A. S., Porta, G., & Payne, M. W. (2012). Longitudinal effects of parental bereavement on adolescent developmental competence. *Journal of Clinical Child & Adolescent Psychology*, 41(6), 778–791.

Brooten, D. A., Youngblut, J. M., Roche, R. M., Caicedo, C. L., & Page, T. F. (2018). Surviving siblings' illnesses, treatments/health services over 13 months after a sibling's death. *Journal of Child and Family Studies*, 27(6), 2049–2056.

Brown, E. J. & Goodman, R. F. (2005). Childhood traumatic grief: An exploration of the construct in children bereaved on September 11. *Journal of Clinical Child and Adolescent Psychology*, 34(2), 248–259.

Burns, R. A., Browning, C. J., & Kendig, H. L. (2015). Examining the 16-year trajectories of mental health and wellbeing through the transition into widowhood. *International Psychogeriatrics*, 27(12), 1979–1986.

Burrell, L. V., Mehlum, L., & Qin, P. (2020). Educational attainment in offspring bereaved by sudden parental death from external causes: A national cohort study from birth and throughout adulthood. *Social Psychiatry and Psychiatric Epidemiology*, 55(6), 779–788.

Burrell, L. V., Mehlum, L., & Qin, P. (2022). Parental death by external causes during childhood and risk of psychiatric disorders in bereaved offspring. *Child and Adolescent Mental Health*, 27(2), 122–130. https://doi.org/10.1111/camh.12470.

Bylund-Grenklo, T., Birgisdóttir, D., Beernaert, K., Nyberg, T., *et al.* (2021). Acute and long-term grief reactions and experiences in parentally cancer-bereaved teenagers. *BMC Palliative Care*, 20(1), 75.

Bylund-Grenklo, T. B., Kreicbergs, U. C., Valdimarsdottir, U. A., Nyberg, T., Steineck, G., & Fürst, C. J. (2013). Communication and trust in the care provided to a dying parent: A nationwide study of cancer-bereaved youths. *Journal of Clinical Oncology*, 31(23), 2886–2894.

Bylund-Grenklo, T., Kreicbergs, U., Valdimarsdóttir, U. A., Nyberg, T., Steineck, G., & Fürst, C. J. (2014). Self-injury in youths who lost a parent to cancer: Nationwide study of the impact of family-related and health-care-related factors. *Psycho-Oncology*. 23(9), 989–997. https://doi.org/10.1002/pon.3515.

Bylund-Grenklo, T. B., Fürst, C. J., Nyberg, T., Steineck, G., & Kreicbergs, U. (2016). Unresolved grief and its consequences: A nationwide follow-up of teenage loss of a parent to cancer 6–9 years earlier. *Supportive Care in Cancer*, 24(7), 3095–3103.

Calderon, S., Samstag, L. W., Papouchis, N., & Saunders, B. A. (2019). The effects of early parental death and grief on interpersonal functioning and alexithymia in adults. *Psychopathology*, 52(3), 198–204.

Chen, C. Y.-C. & Panebianco, A. (2018). Interventions for young bereaved children: A systematic review and implications for school mental health providers. *Child & Youth Care Forum*, 47(2), 151–171. https://doi.org/10.1007/s10566-017-9426-x.

Clabburn, O., Knighting, K., Jack, B. A., & O'Brien, M. R. (2021). Continuing bonds with children and bereaved young people: A narrative review. *OMEGA – Journal of Death and Dying*, 83(3), 371–389. https://doi.org/10.1177/0030222819853195.

Cohen, J. A. & Mannarino, A. P. (2011). Trauma-focused CBT for traumatic grief in military children. *Journal of Contemporary Psychotherapy*, 41(4), 219–227.

Cohen, J. A., Mannarino, A. P., & Knudsen, K. (2004). Treating childhood traumatic grief: A pilot study. *Journal of the American Academy of Child and Adolescent Psychiatry*, 43(10), 1225–1233.

Cohen, J. A., Mannarino, A. P., & Staron, V. R. (2006). A pilot study of modified cognitive-behavioral therapy for childhood traumatic grief (CBT-CTG). *Journal of the American Academy of Child and Adolescent Psychiatry*, 45(12), 1465–1473.

Coleman, J. (1978). Current contradictions in adolescent theory. *Journal of Youth and Adolescence*, 7(1), 1–11.

Coleman, J. (2011). *The Nature of Adolescence* (fourth edition). London: Taylor & Francis.

Cross, S. (ed.) (2002). 'I can't stop feeling sad': Calls to ChildLine about bereavement. ChildLine.

Csikszentmihalyi, M. (1997). *Finding Flow: The Psychology of Engagement with Everyday Life*. New York, NY: Basic Books.

Cuddy-Casey, M. & Orvaschel, H. (1997). Children's understanding of death in relation to child suicidality and homicidality. *Clinical Psychology Review*, 17(1), 33–45.

Dawson, K. S., Joscelyne, A., Meijer, C., Tampubolon, A., Steel, Z., & Bryant, R. A. (2014). Predictors of chronic posttraumatic response in Muslim children following natural disaster. *Psychological Trauma: Theory, Research, Practice, and Policy*, 6(5), 580–587.

De Goede, I. H., Branje, S. J., & Meeus, W. H. (2009). Developmental changes and gender differences in adolescents' perceptions of friendships. *Journal of Adolescence*, 32(5), 1105–1123.

Denes-Raj, V. & Ehrlichman, H. (1991). Effects of premature parental death on subjective life expectancy, death anxiety, and health behaviour. *OMEGA – Journal of Death and Dying*, 23(4), 309–321.

Dietz, L. J., Stoyak, S., Melhem, N., Porta, G., *et al.* (2013). Cortisol response to social stress in parentally bereaved youth. *Biological Psychiatry*, 73(4), 379–387.

Doka, K. J. (ed.) (2013). *Living with Grief: Children, Adolescents and Loss*. London: Routledge.

Dowdney, L. (2000). Annotation: Childhood bereavement following parental death. *Journal of Child Psychology and Psychiatry*, 41(7), 819–830.

Dyregrov, A. (1988). Responding to traumatic stress situations in Europe: Crisis intervention following a multiple murder. *Bereavement Care*, 7(1), 6–9.

Dyregrov, A. (2010). *Supporting Traumatized Children and Teenagers*. London: Jessica Kingsley Publishers.

Dyregrov, A. (2018). *Katastrofepsykologi* (3. utg.) [*Disaster Psychology* (third edition)]. Bergen: Fagbokforlaget.

Dyregrov, A. & Dyregrov, K. (2012). 'Complicated Grief in Children.' In M. Stroebe, H. Schut, & J. Bout (eds), *Complicated Grief: Scientific Foundations for Health Care Professionals* (pp.68–81). New York, NY: Routledge.

Dyregrov, A. & Dyregrov, K. (2013). Complicated grief in children – the perspectives of experienced professionals. *OMEGA – Journal of Death and Dying*, 67(3), 291–303.

Dyregrov, A. & Dyregrov, K. (2016). Barn som mister foreldre. [Children who lose parents.] *Scandinavian Psychologist*, 3, e9.

Dyregrov, A., Bie Wikander, A. M., & Vigerust, S. (1999a). Sudden death of a classmate and friend: Adolescents' perception of support from their school. *School Psychology International*, 20(2), 191–208.

Dyregrov, A., Gjestad, R., Bie Wikander, A. M., & Vigerust, S. (1999b). Reactions following the sudden death of a classmate. *Scandinavian Journal of Psychology*, 40(3), 167–176.

Dyregrov, A., Dyregrov, K., Endsjø, M., & Idsoe, T. (2015a). Teachers' perception of bereaved children's academic performance. *Advances in School Mental Health Promotion*, 8(3), 1–12.

Dyregrov, A., Salloum, A., Kristensen, P., & Dyregrov, K. (2015b). Grief and traumatic grief in children in the context of mass trauma. *Current Psychiatry Reports*, 17(6), 48. https://doi.org/10.1007/s11920-015-0577-x.

Dyregrov, A., Dyregrov, K., Straume, M., & Grønvold Bugge, R. (2016). Weekend family gatherings for bereaved after the terror killings in Norway in 2011. *Bereavement Care*, 35(1), 22–30.

Dyregrov, A., Djup, H. W., Barrett, A., Watkins, J., & Karki, F. U. (2019). Learning from a decade of terror in European cities: Immediate, intermediate, and long-term follow-up. *Scandinavian Psychologist*, 6, e10.

Dyregrov, A., Dyregrov, K., & Lytje, M. (2020b). Loss in the family – A reflection on how schools can support their students. *Bereavement Care*, 39(3), 95–101.

Dyregrov, A., Dyregrov, K., Pereira, M., Kristensen, P., & Johnsen, I. (2020a). Early intervention for bereaved children: What mental health professionals think. *Death Studies*, 44(4), 201–209. https://doi.org/10.1080/07481187.2018.1531086.

Dyregrov, A. & Kristensen, P. (2020). Information to bereaved families following catastrophic losses. Why is it important? *Journal of Loss and Trauma*, 25(2), 1–16.

Dyregrov, K. & Dyregrov, A. (2005). Siblings after suicide – 'The forgotten bereaved'. *Suicide and Life Threatening Behaviour*, 35, 714–724. doi.org/10.1521/suli.2005.35.6.714.

Dyregrov, K. & Dyregrov, A. (2008). *Effective Grief and Bereavement Support: The Role of Family, Friends, Colleagues, Schools and Support Professionals.* London: Jessica Kingsley Publishers.

Dyregrov, K. & Dyregrov, A. (2011). Barn og unge som pårørende ved kreft: Hvordan kan barns situasjon og foreldres omsorgskapasitet styrkes i et rehabiliteringsperspektiv? [Children and youth as relatives in cancer: How can the situation of children and the caregiving capacity of parents be strengthened from a rehabilitation perspective?] Report. Centre for Crisis Psychology.

Dyregrov, K., Dyregrov, A., & Kristensen, P. (2014). Traumatic bereavement and terror: The psychosocial impact on parents and siblings 1.5 years after the July 2011 terror-killings in Norway. *Journal of Loss and Trauma*, 20, 556–576.

Dyregrov, K., Dyregrov, A., & Kristensen, P. (2016). In what ways do bereaved parents after terror go on with their lives, and what seems to inhibit or promote adaptation during their grieving process? A qualitative study. *OMEGA – Journal of Death and Dying*, 73(4), 374–399.

Ellis, J., Dowrick, C., & Lloyd-Williams, M. (2013). The long-term impact of early parental death: Lessons from a narrative study. *Journal of the Royal Society of Medicine*, 106(2), 57–67.

Ennis, J. & Majid, U. (2021). 'Death from a broken heart': A systematic review of the relationship between spousal bereavement and physical and physiological health outcomes. *Death Studies*, 45(7), 538–551. doi: 10.1080/07481187.2019.1661884.

Ennis, N., Pastrana, F. A., Moreland, A. D., Davies, F., delMas, S., & Rheingold, A. (2022). Assessment tools for children who experience traumatic loss: A systematic review. *Trauma, Violence & Abuse*, 15248380221127256. https://doi.org/10.1177/15248380221127256.

Funk, A. M., Jenkins, S., Astroth, K. S., Braswell, G., & Kerber, C. (2018). A narrative analysis of sibling grief. *Journal of Loss and Trauma*, 23(1), 1–14.

Gersten, J. C., Beals, J., & Kallgren, C. A. (1991). Epidemiology and preventive interventions: Parental death in childhood as a case example. *American Journal of Community Psychology*, 19(4), 481–500.

Goenjian, A. K., Walling, D., Steinberg, A. M., Roussos, A., Goenjian, H. A., & Pynoos, R. S. (2009). Depression and PTSD symptoms among bereaved adolescents $6\frac{1}{2}$ years after the 1998 Spitak earthquake. *Journal of Affective Disorders*, 112(1–3), 81–84.

Götze, H., Brahler, E., Gansera, L., Schnabel, A., Gottschalk-Fleischer, A., & Kohler, N. (2018). Anxiety, depression and quality of life in family caregivers of palliative cancer patients during home care and after the patient's death. *European Journal of Cancer Care*, 27(2), e12606.

Granqvist, P., Sroufe, L. A., Dozier, M., Hesse, E., *et al.* (2017). Disorganized attachment in infancy: A review of the phenomenon and its implications for clinicians and policy-makers. *Attachment & Human Development*, 19(6), 534–558.

Gray, L. B., Weller, R. A., Fristad, M., & Weller, E. B. (2011). Depression in children and adolescents two months after the death of a parent. *Journal of Affective Disorders*, 135(1), 277–283.

Green, E. J. & Connolly, M. E. (2009). Jungian family sandplay with bereaved children: Implications for play therapists. *International Journal of Play Therapy*, 18(2), 84.

Guldin, M., Li, J., Pedersen, H., Obel, C., *et al.* (2015). Incidence of suicide among persons who had a parent who died during their childhood: A population-based cohort study. *JAMA Psychiatry*, 72(12), 1227–1234.

Gupta, S. & Bonanno, G. A. (2011). Complicated grief and deficits in emotional expressive flexibility. *Journal of Abnormal Psychology*, 120(3), 635–643.

Hagan, M. J., Roubinov, D. S., Gress-Smith, J., Luecken, L. J., Sandler, I. N., & Wolchik, S. (2011). Positive parenting during childhood moderates the impact of recent negative events on cortisol activity in parentally bereaved youth. *Psychopharmacology*, 214(1), 231–238.

Haine, R. A., Wolchik, S. A., Sandler, I. N., Millsap, R. E., & Ayers, T. S. (2006). Positive parenting as a protective resource for parentally bereaved children. *Death Studies*, 30(1), 1–28.

Hajal, N. J. & Paley, B. (2020). Parental emotion and emotion regulation: A critical target of study for research and intervention to promote child emotion socialization. *Developmental Psychology*, 56(3), 403–417.

Hilliard, R. E. (2007). The effects of Orff-based music therapy and social work groups on childhood grief symptoms and behaviours. *Journal of Music Therapy*, 44(2), 123–138.

Hiyoshi, A., Berg, L., Grotta, A., Almquist, Y., & Rostila, M. (2021). Parental death in childhood and pathways to increased mortality across the life course in Stockholm, Sweden: A cohort study. *PLoS Medicine*, 18(3), e1003549. https://doi.org/10.1371/journal.pmed.1003549.

Hogan, N. S. & DeSantis, L. (1994). Things that help and hinder adolescent sibling bereavement. *Western Journal of Nursing Research*, 16(2), 132–146.

Holland, J. (1993). Child bereavement in Humberside primary schools. *Educational Research*, 35(3), 289–297.

Holland, J. (2000). Secondary schools and pupil loss by parental bereavement and parental relationship separations. *Pastoral Care in Education*, 18(4), 33–39.

Holland, J. (2003). Supporting schools with loss: 'Lost for Words' in Hull. *British Journal of Special Education*, 30(2), 76–78.

Holmgren, H. (2021). Life came to a full stop: The experiences of widowed fathers. *OMEGA – Journal of Death and Dying*, 84(1), 126–145. https://doi.org/10.1177/0030222819880713.

Howell, K. H., Barrett-Becker, E. P., Burnside, A. N., Wamser-Nanney, R., Layne, C. M., & Kaplow, J. B. (2016). Children facing parental cancer versus parental death: The buffering effects of positive parenting and emotional expression. *Journal of Child and Family Studies*, 25(1), 152–164.

Hunter, S. B. & Smith, D. E. (2008). Predictors of children's understandings of death: Age, cognitive ability, death experience and maternal communicative competence. *OMEGA – Journal of Death and Dying*, 57(2), 143–162.

Høeg, B. L., Appel, C. W., von Heymann-Horan, A. B., Frederiksen, K., *et al.* (2017). Maladaptive coping in adults who have experienced early parental loss and grief counseling. *Journal of Health Psychology*, 22(14), 1851–1861.

Høeg, B. L., Johansen, C., Christensen, J., Frederiksen, K., *et al.* (2018). Early parental loss and intimate relationships in adulthood: A nationwide study. *Developmental Psychology*, 54(5), 963–974.

Høeg, B. L., Christensen, J., Frederiksen, K., Dalton, S. O., *et al.* (2019). Does losing a parent early influence the education you obtain? A nationwide cohort study in Denmark. *Journal of Public Health*, 41(2), 296–304.

Høeg, B. L., Christensen, J., Banko, L., Frederiksen, K., *et al.* (2023). Psychotropic medication among children who experience parental death to cancer. *European Child & Adolescent Psychiatry*, 32(1), 155–165. https://doi.org/10.1007/s00787-021-01846-y.

Jabre, P., Belpomme, V., Azoulay, E., Jacob, L., *et al.* (2013). Family presence during cardiopulmonary resuscitation. *New England Journal of Medicine*, 368(11), 1008–1018.

Jørgensen, S. E., Andersen, A., Lund, L., Due, P., & Michelsen, S. I. (2019). Trivsel og hverdagsliv blandt børn og unge som pårørende og efterladte [Well-being and daily life among children and young people as relatives and bereaved]. Statens Institut for Folkesundhed.

Kailaheimo-Lönnqvist, S. & Kotimäki, S. (2020). Cause of parental death and child's health and education: The role of parental resources. *SSM – Population Health*, 11, 100632.

Kalantari, M. & Vostanis, P. (2010). Behavioural and emotional problems in Iranian children four years after parental death in an earthquake. *International Journal of Social Psychiatry*, 56(2), 158–167.

Kaplow, J. B., Howell, K. H., & Layne, C. M. (2014). Do circumstances of the death matter? Identifying socioenvironmental risks for grief-related psychopathology in bereaved youth. *Journal of Traumatic Stress*, 27(1), 42–49.

Kennedy, B., Chen, R., Valdimarsdottir, U., Montgomery, S., Fang, F., & Fall, K. (2018). Childhood bereavement and lower stress resilience in late adolescence. *Journal of Adolescent Health*, 63(1), 108–114.

Keulen, J., Spuij, M., Deković, M., & Boelen, P. A. (2022). Heterogeneity of post-traumatic stress symptoms in bereaved children and adolescents: Exploring subgroups and possible risk factors. *Psychiatry Research*, 312, 114575. https://doi.org/10.1016/j.psychres.2022.114575.

Kivimäki, M. & Steptoe, A. (2018). Effects of stress on the development and progression of cardiovascular disease. *Nature Reviews Cardiology*, 15(4), 215–229. https://doi.org/10.1038/nrcardio.2017.189.

Kranzler, E. M., Shaffer, D., Wasserman, G., & Davies, M. (1990). Early childhood bereavement. *Journal of the American Academy of Child and Adolescent Psychiatry*, 29(4), 513–520.

Krattenmacher, T., Kuhne, F., Fuhrer, D., Beierlein, V., et al. (2013). Coping skills and mental health status in adolescents when a parent has cancer: A multicenter and multi-perspective study. *Journal of Psychosomatic Research*, 74(3), 252–259.

Kristensen, P., Dyregrov, K., & Dyregrov, A. (2017). Can visiting the site of death be beneficial for bereaved families after terror? A qualitative study of parents' and siblings' experiences of visiting Utøya Island after the 2011 Norway terror attack. *European Journal of Psychotraumatology*, 8(sup6). doi: 10.1080/20008198.2018.1463795.

Kristensen, P., Dyregrov, A., & Dyregrov, K. (2021). *Sorg og komplisert sorg [Grief and Complicated Grief]*. Bergen: Fagbokforlaget.

Layne, C. M., Pynoos, R. S., Saltzman, W. R., Arslanagić, B., et al. (2001). Trauma/grief-focused group psychotherapy: School-based postwar intervention with traumatized Bosnian adolescents. *Group Dynamics: Theory, Research, and Practice*, 5(4), 277–290.

Layne, C. M., Saltzman, W. R., Poppleton, L., Burlingame, G. M., et al. (2008). Effectiveness of a school-based group psychotherapy program for war-exposed adolescents: A randomized controlled trial. *Journal of the American Academy of Child and Adolescent Psychiatry*, 47(9), 1048–1062.

Layne, C. M., Greeson, J. K. P., Ostrowski, S. A., Kim, S., et al. (2014). Cumulative trauma exposure and high risk behaviour in adolescence: Findings from the NCTSN Core Data Set. *Psychological Trauma: Theory, Research, Practice, and Policy*, 6(S1), S40–S49.

Li, D.-J., Tsai, S.-J., Chen, T.-J., Liang, C.-S., & Chen, M.-H. (2022). Risks of major mental disorders after parental death in children, adolescents, and young adults and the role of premorbid mental comorbidities: A population-based cohort study. *Social Psychiatry and Psychiatric Epidemiology*, 57(12), 2393–2400. https://doi.org/10.1007/s00127-022-02334-7.

Li, J., Vestergaard, M., Cnattingius, S., Gissler, M., et al. (2014). Mortality after parental death in childhood: A nationwide cohort study from three Nordic countries. *PLoS Medicine*, 11(7), 1–13.

Li, Y., Chan, W. C. H., & Marrable, T. (2023). 'I never told my family I was griev-ing for my mom': The not-disclosing-grief experiences of parentally bereaved adolescents and young adults in Chinese families. *Family Process*. https://doi.org/10.1111/famp.12865.

Lin, K. K., Sandler, I. N., Ayers, T. S., Wolchik, S. A., & Luecken, L. J. (2004). Resilience in parentally bereaved children and adolescents seeking preventive services. *Journal of Clinical Child & Adolescent Psychology*, 33(4), 673–683.

Linder, L., Lunardini, M., & Zimmerman, H. (2022). Supporting childhood bereave-ment through school-based grief group. *OMEGA – Journal of Death and Dying*. https://doi.org/10.1177/00302228221082756.

Liu, M., Wang, L., Shi, Z., Zhang, Z., Zhang, K., & Shen, J. (2011). Mental health prob-lems among children one-year after Sichuan earthquake in China: A follow-up study. *PLOS One*, 6(2), e14706.

Liu, X., Olsen, J., Agerbo, E., Yuan, W., Cnattingius, S., Gissler, M. & Li, J. (2013). Psychological stress and hospitalization for childhood asthma – A nationwide cohort study in two Nordic countries. *PLOS One*, 8(10), e78816.

Lövgren, M., Sveen, J., Steineck, G., Wallin, A. E., Eilertsen, M.-E. B., & Kreicbergs, U. (2019). Spirituality and religious coping are related to cancer-bereaved siblings' long-term grief. *Palliative & Supportive Care*, 7(2), 138–142. doi:10.1017/S1478951517001146..

Lowton, K. & Higginson, I. J. (2003). Managing bereavement in the classroom: A conspiracy of silence? *Death Studies*, 27(8), 717–741.

Luecken, L. J. (2008). Long-term consequences of parental death in childhood: Psy-chological and physiological manifestations. In I. M. S. Stroebe, R. O. Hansson, W. Stroebe, & H. Schut (eds), *Handbook of Bereavement Research and Practice: Advances in Theory and Intervention* (s.397–416). Washington, DC: American Psy-chological Association.

Luecken, L. J. & Roubinov, D. S. (2012). Pathways to lifespan health following child-hood parental death. *Social and Personality Psychology Compass*, 6(3), 243–257.

Luecken, L. J., Kraft, A., Appelhans, B. M., & Enders, C. (2009). Emotional and cardiovascular sensitization to daily stress following childhood parental loss. *Developmental Psychology*, 45(1), 296–302.

Lytje, M. (2016a). Unheard Voices: Parentally Bereaved Danish Students' Experiences and Perceptions of the Support Received Following the Return to School. Doc-toral dissertation, University of Cambridge.

Lytje, M. (2016b). Voices we forget – Danish students' experience of returning to school following parental bereavement. *OMEGA – Journal of Death and Dying*, 78(1), 24–42.

Lytje, M. (2017). Voices that want to be heard – Using bereaved Danish students' suggestions to update school bereavement response plans. *Death Studies*, 42(4), 254–276.

Lytje, M. & Dyregrov, A. (2019). The price of loss – A literature review of the psy-chosocial and health consequences of childhood bereavement. *Bereavement Care*, 38(1), 13–22.

Lytje, M. & Dyregrov, A. (2021). When young children grieve: Supporting daycare children following bereavement – A parent's perspective. *OMEGA – Journal of Death and Dying*, 86(3), 980–1001. https://doi.org/10.1177/0030222821997702.

Mack, K. Y. (2001). Childhood family disruptions and adult well-being: The differ-ential effects of divorce and parental death. *Death Studies*, 25(5), 419–443.

Malone, P. A. (2012). The impact of peer death on adolescent girls: An efficacy study of the Adolescent Grief and Loss group. *Social Work with Groups*, 35(1), 35–49.

Manzoni, M., Fernandez, I., Bertella, S., Tizzoni, F., *et al.* (2021). Eye movement desensitization and reprocessing: The state of the art of efficacy in children and adolescents with post-traumatic stress disorder. *Journal of Affective Disorders*, 282, 340–347.

Martinčeková, L., Jiang, M. J., Adams, J. D., Menendez, D., *et al.* (2020). Do you remember being told what happened to Grandma? The role of early socialization on later coping with death. *Death Studies*, 44(2), 78–88. https://doi.org/10.1080/0 7481187.2018.1522386.

Masterson, M. P., Schuler, T. A., & Kissane, D. W. (2013). Family focused grief therapy: A versatile intervention in palliative care and bereavement. *Bereavement Care*, 32(3), 117–123.

McClatchy, I. S., Vonk, M. E., & Palardy, G. (2009). The prevalence of childhood traumatic grief – A comparison of violent/sudden and expected loss. *OMEGA – Journal of Death and Dying*, 59(4), 305–323.

Melhem, N. M., Walker, M., Moritz, G., & Brent, D. A. (2008). Antecedents and sequelae of sudden parental death in offspring and surviving caregivers. *Archives of Pediatrics & Adolescent Medicine*, 162(5), 403–410.

Melhem, N. M., Porta, G., Shamseddeen, W., Walker Payne, M. & Brent, D. A. (2011). Grief in children and adolescents bereaved by sudden parental death. *Archives of General Psychiatry*, 68(9), 911–919.

Merz, C. J. & Wolf, O. T. (2022). How stress hormones shape memories of fear and anxiety in humans. *Neuroscience and Biobehavioral Reviews*, 142, 104901.

Niederkrotenthaler, T., Floderus, B., Alexanderson, K., Rasmussen, F., & Mittendorfer-Rutz, E. (2012). Exposure to parental mortality and markers of morbidity, and the risks of attempted and completed suicide in offspring: An analysis of sensitive life periods. *Journal of Epidemiological Community Health*, 66(3), 233–239.

Nielsen, J. C., Sorensen, N. U., & Hansen, N. M. (2012). *Unge pårørende og efterladtes trivsel [Young Relatives and Survivors' Well-Being]*. Aarhus Universitet.

Oltjenbruns, K. A. (1991). Positive outcomes of adolescents' experience with grief. *Journal of Adolescent Research*, 6(1), 43–53. https://doi.org/10.1177/074355489161004.

Omerov, P., Pettersen, R., Titelman, D., Nyberg, T., *et al.* (2017). Encountering the body at the site of the suicide: A population-based survey in Sweden. *Suicide & Life-Threatening Behaviour*, 47(1), 38–47.

Otowa, T., York, T. P., Gardner, C. O., Kendler, K. S., & Hettema, J. M. (2014). The impact of childhood parental loss on risk for mood, anxiety and substance use disorders in a population-based sample of male twins. *Psychiatry Research*, 220(1–2), 404–409.

Parsons, S. (2011). *Long-term impact of parental bereavement: Preliminary analysis of the 1970 British cohort study (BCS70)*. London: Childhood Wellbeing Research Centre.

Pereira, M., Johnsen, I., Hauken, M. A., Kristensen, P., & Dyregrov, A. (2017). Early interventions following the death of a parent: Protocol of a mixed methods systematic review. *JMIR Research Protocols*, 6(6), e127.

Pfefferbaum, B., North, C. S., Doughty, D. E., Pfefferbaum, R. L., *et al.* (2006). Trauma, grief and depression in Nairobi children after the 1998 bombing of the American embassy. *Death Studies*, 30(6), 561–577.

Pham, S., Porta, G., Biernesser, C., Walker Payne, M., *et al.* (2018). The burden of bereavement: Early-onset depression and impairment in youths bereaved by sudden parental death in a 7-year prospective study. *The American Journal of Psychiatry*, 175(9), 887–896.

Poijula, S., Dyregrov, A., Wahlberg, K. E., & Jokelainen, J. (2001). Reactions to adolescent suicide and crisis intervention in three secondary schools. *International Journal of Emergency Mental Health*, 3(2), 97–106.

Prix, I. & Erola, J. (2017). Does death really make us equal? Educational attainment and resource compensation after paternal death in Finland. *Social Science Research*, 64, 171–183.

Pynoos, R. S. (1992). Grief and trauma in children and adolescents. *Bereavement Care*, 11(1), 2–10.

Reinherz, H. Z., Giaconia, R. M., Hauf, A. M., Wasserman, M. S., & Silverman, A. B. (1999). Major depression in the transition to adulthood: Risks and impairments. *Journal of Abnormal Psychology*, 108(3), 500–510.

Ribbens McCarthy, J. with Jessop, J. (2005). *Young People, Bereavement and Loss: Disruptive Transitions?* London: Joseph Rowntree Foundation/National Children's Bureau.

Riches, G. & Dawson, P. (2000). Daughters' dilemma: Grief resolution in girls whose widowed fathers remarry early. *Journal of Family Therapy*, 22(4), 360–374.

Rose, A. J. & Rudolph, K. D. (2006). A review of sex differences in peer relationship processes: Potential trade-offs for the emotional and behavioural development of girls and boys. *Psychological Bulletin*, 132(1), 98–131.

Rostila, M. & Saarela, J. M. (2011). Time does not heal all wounds: Mortality following the death of a parent. *Journal of Marriage and Family*, 73(1), 236–249.

Rostila, M., Berg, L., Arat, A., Vinnerljung, B., & Hjern, A. (2016). Parental death in childhood and self-inflicted injuries in young adults – A national cohort study from Sweden. *European Child & Adolescent Psychiatry*, 25(10), 1103–1111.

Rostila, M., Berg, L., Saarela, J., Kawachi, I., & Hjern, A. (2017). Experience of sibling death in childhood and risk of death in adulthood: A national cohort study from Sweden. *American Journal of Epidemiology*, 185(12), 1247–1254.

Saldinger, A., Porterfield, K., & Cain, A. C. (2004). Meeting the needs of parentally bereaved children: A framework for child-centered parenting. *Psychiatry*, 67(4), 331–352.

Salloum, A. & Overstreet, S. (2008). Evaluation of individual and group grief and trauma interventions for children post disaster. *Journal of Clinical Child & Adolescent Psychology*, 37(3), 495–507.

Sandler, I., Gunn, H., Mazza, G., Tein, J.-Y., *et al.* (2018). Three perspectives on mental health problems of young adults and their parents at a 15-year follow-up of the family bereavement program. *Journal of Consulting and Clinical Psychology*, 86(10), 845–855.

Sandler, I., Yun-Tien, J., Zhang, N., Wolchik, S., & Thieleman, K. (2021). Grief as a predictor of long-term risk for suicidal ideation and attempts of parentally bereaved children and adolescents. *Journal of Traumatic Stress*, 34(6), 1159–1170. https://doi.org/10.1002/jts.22759.

Schepers, S. A. (2019). Commentary – Fifty years of development in pediatric psycho-oncology research and practice: How far have we come? *Journal of Pediatric Psychology*, 44(7), 761–763.

Schonfeld, D. J., Demaria, T., & Committee on Psychosocial Aspects of Child and Family Health, Disaster Preparedness Advisory Council (2016). Supporting the grieving child and family. *Pediatrics*, 138(3), e20162147.

Servaty-Seib, H. L. & Pistole, M. C. (2007). Adolescent grief: Relationship category and emotional closeness. *OMEGA – Journal of Death and Dying*, 54(2), 147–167. https://doi.org/10.2190/M002-1541-JP28-4673.

Shapiro, F. & Laliotis, D. (2011). EMDR and the adaptive information processing model: Integrative treatment and case conceptualization. *Clinical Social Work Journal*, 39(2), 191–200.

Shapiro, D. N., Howell, K. H., & Kaplow, J. B. (2014). Associations among mother-child communication quality, childhood maladaptive grief, and depressive symptoms. *Death Studies*, 38(3), 172–178.

Sheehan, D. K., Hansen, D., Stephenson, P., Mayo, M., Albataineh, R., & Anaba, E. (2019). Telling adolescents that a parent has died. *Journal of Hospice & Palliative Nursing*, 21(2), 152–159. https://doi.org/10.1097/NJH.0000000000000506.

Shulla, R. M. & Toomey, R. B. (2018). Sex differences in behavioural and psychological expression of grief during adolescence: A meta-analysis. *Journal of Adolescence*, 65, 219–227.

Sirrine, E. H., Salloum, A., & Boothroyd, R. (2018). Predictors of continuing bonds among bereaved adolescents. *OMEGA – Journal of Death and Dying*, 76(3), 237–255. https://doi.org/10.1177/0030222817727632.

Slaughter, V. (2005). Young children's understanding of death. *Australian Psychologist*, 40(3), 179–186.

Smith, K. R., Hanson, H. A., Norton, M. C., Hollingshaus, M. S., & Mineau, G. P. (2014). Survival of offspring who experience early parental death: Early life conditions and later-life mortality. *Social Science & Medicine*, 119, 180–190. https://doi.org/10.1016/j.socscimed.2013.11.054.

Spuij, M., Reitz, E., Prinzie, P., Stikkelbroek, Y., de Roos, C., & Boelen, P. A. (2012). Distinctiveness of symptoms of prolonged grief, depression, and posttraumatic stress in bereaved children and adolescents. *European Child & Adolescent Psychiatry*, 21(12), 673–679.

Spuij, M., Deković, M., & Boelen, P. A. (2013). An open trial of 'grief-help': A cognitive-behavioural treatment for prolonged grief in children and adolescents. *Clinical Psychology & Psychotherapy*, 22(2), 185–192.

Stikkelbroek, Y., Bodden, D. H., Reitz, E., Vollebergh, W. A., & van Baar, A. L. (2016). Mental health of adolescents before and after the death of a parent or sibling. *European Child & Adolescent Psychiatry*, 25(1), 49–59.

Straume, M. (1999). Sorggrupper for barn som har mistet sosken av kreft [Bereavement groups for children who have lost siblings to cancer]. *Tidsskrift for Norsk psykologforening*, 36, 107–115.

Stroebe, M. S. & Schut, H. (1999). The dual process model of coping with bereavement: Rationale and description. *Death Studies*, 23(3), 197–224.

Tang, B., Liu, X., Liu, Y., Xue, C., & Zhang, L. (2014). A meta-analysis of risk factors for depression in adults and children after natural disasters. *BMC Public Health*, 14(1), 623.

Tremblay, G. C. & Israel, A. C. (1998). Children's adjustment to parental death. *Clinical Psychology: Science and Practice*, 5(4), 424–438.

Turunen, T. & Punamäki, R.-L. (2014). Psychosocial support for trauma-affected students after school shootings in Finland. *Violence and Victims*, 29(3), 476–491.

Usami, M., Iwadare, Y., Watanabe, K., Kodaira, M., *et al.* (2014). Prosocial behaviours during school activities among child survivors after the 2011 earthquake and Tsunami in Japan: A retrospective observational study. *PLOS One*, 9(11), e113709.

Vaccarino, V., Almuwaqqat, Z., Kim, J. H., Hammadah, M., *et al.* (2021). Association of mental stress-induced myocardial ischemia with cardiovascular events in patients with coronary heart disease. *JAMA*, 326(18), 1818–1828. https://doi.org/10.1001/jama.2021.17649.

Van Eerdewegh, M. M., Clayton, P. J., & Van Eerdewegh, P. (1985). The bereaved child: Variables influencing early psychopathology. *British Journal of Psychiatry*, 147(2), 188.

van Praag, H. M. (2004). Can stress cause depression? *Progress in Neuro-Psychopharmacology and Biological Psychiatry*, 28(5), 891–907. https://doi.org/10.1016/j.pnpbp.2004.05.031.

Virk, J., Ritz, B., Li, J., Obel, C., & Olsen, J. (2016). Childhood bereavement and type 1 diabetes: A Danish National Register Study. *Paediatric and Perinatal Epidemiology*, 30(1), 86–92. https://doi.org/10.1111/ppe.12247.

Wells, A. & Sembi, S. (2004). Metacognitive therapy for PTSD: A preliminary investigation of a new brief treatment. *Journal of Behaviour Therapy and Experimental Psychiatry*, 35(4), 307–318.

Widen, S. C. & Russell, J. A. (2010). Differentiation in preschooler's categories of emotion. *Emotion*, 10(5), 651–661.

Winther-Lindqvist, D. A. & Olund Larsen, I. (2021). Grief and best friendship among adolescent girls. *OMEGA – Journal of Death and Dying*, 83(3), 545–562. https://doi.org/10.1177/0030222819856146.

Wolchik, S. A., Coxe, S., Tein, J. Y., Sandler, I. N., & Ayers, T. S. (2008). Six-year longitudinal predictors of posttraumatic growth in parentally bereaved adolescents and young adults. *OMEGA – Journal of Death and Dying*, 58(2), 107–128.

Worden, J. W. (1996). *Children and Grief: When a Parent Dies*. New York, NY: Guilford Press.

World Health Organization. (2018). *International Classification of Diseases for Mortality and Morbidity Statistics* (11th revision). https://icd.who.int/browse11/l-m/en.

Subject Index

Author Index